RECYCLING SOLID WASTE

RECYCLING SOLID WASTE

The First Choice for Private
and Public Sector Management

Thomas E. Duston

Q Quorum Books
Westport, Connecticut • London

COPYRIGHT ACKNOWLEDGMENTS

Biocycle, The J.G. Press, Inc., 419 State Avenue, Second Floor, Emmaus, Pa., for extracts from Vol. 32, No. 7, July 1991.

King, Lawrence W., "A Technical Study of Municipal Solid Waste Composting and the Effect of Disposable Paper Diapers," September 1991, Procter and Gamble, Cincinnati, Ohio.

The New Hampshire Resource Recovery Association, P.O. Box 721, Concord, New Hampshire, for extracts from *Recycling in New Hampshire: An Implementation Guide*.

Library of Congress Cataloging-in-Publication Data

Duston, Thomas E.
    Recycling solid waste : the first choice for private and public
sector management / Thomas E. Duston.
        p. cm.
    Includes bibliographical references and index.
    ISBN 0-89930-754-X (alk. paper)
    1. Recycling (Waste, etc.) — Planning.   2. Recycling (Waste, etc.) —
Cost effectiveness.   I. Title.
    TD794.5.D85   1993
    363.72'82 — dc20   92-31709

British Library Cataloguing in Publication Data is available.

Library of Congress Catalog Card Number: 92-31709
ISBN: 0-89930-754-X

First published in 1993

Quorum Books, 88 Post Road West, Westport, CT 06881
An imprint of Greenwood Publishing Group, Inc.

Printed in the United States of America

The paper used in this book complies with the
Permanent Paper Standard issued by the National
Information Standards Organization (Z39.48-1984).

10 9 8 7 6 5 4 3 2 1

To Mum and Dad for their continuing adaptability
To Bob for opening a new professional vista to me
and to Paula, who knows why

Contents

Figures and Tables

FIGURES

TABLES

List of Appendixes

Preface

The unabashed purpose of this book is to promote recycling. I don't mean recycling as a group of committed environmentalists with a bunch of 55-gallon drums, nor recycling as an effort by the ninth grade to raise money for its class trip to Washington, D.C. Nor do I refer to recycling as part of what is called *integrated waste management* by commercial interests promoting incineration. My purpose is none of these. Instead it is to show that recycling has come of age and that it can be the first choice for solid waste management in the vast majority of waste disposal situations in the United States. By first choice I mean that a recycling plan, if properly planned and implemented, can often be the least costly method of dealing with most of the material in the solid waste stream. I will show that this is true for many disposal situations, in addition to the common one of residential solid waste. It also can be first choice for the more specialized solid waste found in office buildings, shopping malls, warehouses, schools and colleges, recreation areas, or almost any place where people live, work, or play.

Much of what passes for evidence about recycling is anecdotal. How often do we hear the recycler say, "I have tons of stored newspapers and I can't get rid of it?" This simple statement, or some variant of it, is often used to show that recycling does not pay. This negative conclusion about recycling, what we often call the *recycler's lament*, is based on two crucial but faulty notions about solid waste disposal. The first of these is that revenue from sale is a necessary ingredient of a successful recycling program. This is often not the case, and in fact the major gain from the recycling of most materials (including newspapers) is the costs avoided, the avoidance of the often-significant cost of getting rid of the newspapers as trash. Each ton taken out of the waste stream saves the cost of disposing of that ton as trash, and in some parts of the country this cost is approaching $100. Recycling newspapers in these situations would be worth $100 per ton, even if the newspapers were given away.

The second flaw in the argument that recycling does not pay is based on a misunderstanding of the nature of the solid waste stream. Solid waste is often a collection of diverse materials. It is this very diversity that helps protect recycling programs from temporary softness in the markets for specific items (such as newspapers). Since there is no systematic connection between the markets for paper, glass, plastic, aluminum, and so forth, the fact that newspapers are piling up is unlikely to imply anything about the markets for other materials (or even other types of paper). In fact it is this very diversity that protects the recycling program. The best analogy is to view a comprehensive recycling program as being protected from market risk in the same way that a stock portfolio is protected by diversification.

The book discusses in detail the appropriate way to think about these two crucial issues. As examples of the depth of analysis, Chapter 2 is solely about the anatomy of the solid waste stream and Chapter 4 focuses wholly on the proper accounting method for recyling programs. The case for recycling, as made in these chapters and throughout the book, is meant to be understandable to the reader with only a minimal background in recycling. What the reader needs primarily is an interest in the subject.

Among specific topics covered in the book are

- how to look at a waste stream in a new way — not as waste, but as a collection of useful materials, many of which have market value.

- how to give a recycling program the best chance of success. This is done by explaining how to incorporate processing, materials handling, storage, and monitoring in a plan.

- how to evaluate each material in a solid waste stream in terms of its potential for recycling.

- how to deal in a rational and understandable fashion with the many questions others will pose as one tries to establish a recycling program. Some questions will be technical, some will be economic, and some will generally just be skeptical.

- how to evaluate a recycling program so that efficiency improvements can be made when needed in day-to-day operations.

This evaluation may also enable readers to demonstrate more clearly economic gains from recycling in their own localities. This should help when questions of recycling program expansion arise.

My personal experience with the economics of recycling comes from being part of two generations of recyclers. The forgettable first experience was back in the early 1970s. We collected cans and bottles by cleaning up the sides of roads on Earth Day, but did not know what to do with our barrels of containers. Recycling seemed to be the right thing to do, but substantial problems existed. Processing systems were minimal, markets were unstable, broad public support was lacking, and we were ignorant of the true cost of burying waste in dumps and unlined landfills or burning it in low-tech incinerators.

The second generation of recycling, the modern era, is quite different, as another personal example will show. In March 1988, I was asked to chair a committee that would implement a mandatory recycling program recently approved by an overwhelming majority of voters in the small town of Chesterfield, New Hampshire (population 3,000). In the short space of only two years, the town attained a solid waste disposal budget that was 40 percent smaller than it would have been without recycling. Important ingredients for this success were widespread support from the town, careful research and planning by the town committee, and thorough investigation of recycling programs in place elsewhere. In addition to these local considerations, two much larger developments had taken place since the early 1970s. First, recycling equipment and methods are now widely known and available. Second, although sometimes unreliable, markets do exist for most materials in the solid waste stream. One significant result of doing the numerical analysis for the Chesterfield recycling facility is that I was able to identify the essential elements in a trash-to-market production plan. And it turns out that these essentials could be used in a wide variety of solid waste disposal situations.

It is the perspective of the economist that makes this book unique. I have presented the initial elements of the recycling process to widely diverse groups concerned about solid waste disposal. These groups have ranged from enthusiastic local community people to cautious colleagues in economics to skeptical state business leaders. Most were receptive, and all contributed in various ways to the continuing development of these ideas. In fact, these varied contributions have helped make this book not only technically sound but also useful in practical applications. Specific topics that have been presented to professional audiences from both the Eastern Economics Association and the American Public Health Association include the cost-benefit analysis of recycling, the microeconomics of recycling, and the evaluation of a recycling program.

The material in the book is organized to meet the needs of those people actually setting up recycling plans. Step-by-step guidance is given on how to think about solid waste and how to convert this thinking into a waste disposal system with recycling as the first choice. Although many examples are drawn from New Hampshire and surrounding regions, the material is extensively generalized for widespread use. Recycling is a waste disposal system whose time has come, and I hope that this book will show the reader not only how to do it but how to do it successfully.

Acknowledgments

This book has been strengthened immeasurably through numerous suggestions made to me by colleagues, local officials, waste disposal planners, recycling experts, and participants at various regional and national conventions. At the start there was the Chesterfield Recycling Committee, especially Ed Bergeron, Betty Hickley, Lou Perham, Dave Hall, and Marshall Bills. With a conviction that recycling was the right thing to do and drawing inspiration from the then recently deceased recycling advocate Larry Taylor, we spent the many months necessary to plan a recycling program that would work. Once they saw the light, the selectmen at the time, Kurt Nowill, Liz Benjamin, and Steve Laskowski became strong public advocates for proper funding of the program. Peter Erickson and Susan Armstrong, attendants at Operation LARRY (the Chesterfield Recycling Center), have always been very understanding of my continual search for information about the practical aspects of recycling. Susan Armstrong will be my first choice if they ever ask me to nominate a state director of recycling. Alvin Davis, as director of public works, has shown himself to be a dedicated and creative supporter of recycling. Evelyn Nadeau and Bunny Peakes at the town office were always patient and understanding. I would like to make a special acknowledgment in memory of the always thorough and cheerful help of Administrative Assistant Joan Dittrich, who passed away in 1992.

Thanks also go to Robert Sherry, Emily Northrop, and Lorna Gross, current and former colleagues at Keene State College, for their helpful comments on drafts of the various papers on recycling that this research has generated. I especially want to thank Bob Sherry for his initial encouragement to "go professional" on this subject and his cheerful willingness to read and comment at length on the work at many stages. Thanks go, too, to the students, in number and courses too numerous to mention, who were exposed to more about recycling than they probably ever wanted to know. I would like to make a special note of appreciation to Dean Gordon Leversee for his continuing commitment to provide the means for me and others to make the trips necessary to expose our work to regional and national audiences. To the many, many members of both the Eastern Economics Association and the American Public Health Association, who listened and commented in many different forums, a blanket note of thanks. The staff of the New Hampshire Resource Recovery Association has always been willing to explain something, even to a frequent and often demanding caller. Although Eric Valentine at Quorum Books doesn't understand recycling, I appreciate his help in making me a more concise writer! Thanks for her continual understanding to Caron Nelson at The Bookmakers, Incorporated.

Nancy Gitchell typed the first draft of the manuscript and Brenda Phillips the second. Without their competence, understanding, and interpretive magic, I would not have survived this project — a special note of thanks and appreciation for their efforts and unfailing good humor. Richard Bennett did a great job on the graphics and I appreciate his skill. Many friends and relatives have sent me recycling materials of various sorts. For these I thank Joyce Goggin, Bill Duston, and Sally and Dean Whitlock. A special note of thanks to Allen Padua for his continuing flow of materials on plastics recycling.

For two years I have used writing this book as an excuse not to take on other worthwhile projects: my thanks to friends in Chesterfield and at the college for their patience and understanding in this regard. To my two kids at home, Christopher and Jessie, I thank you for understanding about all those times I could not go fishing or play baseball or go to the beach. I'll make it up to you. And of course my thanks to Paula, who has been a continuing source of understanding, encouragement, and stability, at all those times when either household or professional chaos could have taken over.

1

Introduction

With the costs of solid waste disposal escalating, recycling has become a necessity in many parts of the country. This is true, even allowing that the term *recycling* may have different meanings to different people. Although most of these definitions would be something like taking stuff out of the trash and using it again, a more formal definition, compliments of the U.S. Environmental Protection Agency (EPA) is: "Recycling means separating, collecting, processing, marketing and ultimately using a material that was thrown away" (EPA, 1990).

As a practical matter, recycling programs also may include discarded items such as clothing taken home for reuse, composting of certain organic materials, repair and sale components, and discarded materials changed to different uses. Whatever their scope, recycling programs offer to towns, businesses, hospitals, office buildings, schools and other institutions, and any other producer of solid waste an opportunity to reduce disposal costs *and* do something good for the environment. The problem of what to do with all the newspapers, old tires, tin cans, and garbage has become acute primarily because of the serious political and environmental difficulties that exist with incineration and landfilling, the major systems currently in use for getting rid of trash (i.e., unsorted solid waste). Political difficulties exist because voters do not want landfills or incinerators in their town (the NIMBY phenomenon: Not In My Backyard); hence politically acceptable sites are difficult to find. Environmental problems include air pollution and toxic ash from incineration, as well as groundwater pollution from landfills. Even if these problems have been dealt with, environmentally acceptable sites are still very difficult to find. Given this difficulty, it is not surprising that often the most significant gain from successful recycling is the large reduction in trash volume and therefore a greatly reduced need for incineration and landfilling. Obviously, this also reduces costs accordingly. Since recycling

Table 1.1
Monthly Total of Recyclables as Percentages of Yearly Amount,
10/90–9/91

			MATERIAL		
					Aluminum
				Scrap	& Steel
MONTH	Paper	Glass	Plastics	Metal	Cans
October	8	6	0	12	8
November	8	9	4	16	5
December	7	5	0	8	12
January	9	12	42	3	6
February	8	4	0	5	13
March	7	8	0	5	6
April	6	8	0	8	12
May	9	6	0	10	13
June	10	7	25	12	9
July	8	12	17	7	8
August	12	14	4	8	4
September	9	7	8	5	5

Source: New Hampshire Resource Recovery Association, *1991 Annual Report*, p. 7.

reduces the need for something that is becoming increasingly difficult and costly, it will be shown in this book that recycling is not only the right thing to do, but in a surprising number of cases it is also cost-effective.

The study of recycling confronts many readers with a number of new terms. Appendix 1.1 contains a glossary of commonly used and useful terms.

The reader at this point may also wish to complement the reading of this book with journal articles and simple pamphlets about the major materials that can be recycled. Appendix 1.2 is a list of major solid waste and recycling journals, and Appendix 1.3 contains names and addresses of appropriate material trade associations (aluminum, tin, glass, etc.).

ORGANIZATION OF THE BOOK

Part I, Research and Planning for Recycling, contains Chapters 2 through 4. Since a major theme of this book is that time must be spent in preparation before actually setting up a recycling plan, Part I lays out in detail the planning and investigation steps that should be taken prior to starting a recycling program. Chapter 2 provides the reader with skills for analyzing different solid waste streams. This is done in two ways, first by providing data on typical streams of solid waste. Examples include data from municipalities, from household hazardous waste, and from construction/demolition debris. From these the reader can get a sense of the relative proportions of various items. Second, by identifying several ways of dividing up a waste stream, such as by percentage of each material, ease of handling, and ease of recycling, the reader understands the various dimensions of material diversity in waste streams. This exercise is very helpful because contrary to the common view, those things known as *recycled goods* are often very dissimilar, with collection, processing, and marketing often unique for each material. And, not surprisingly, it is this very diversity of materials that often can protect a comprehensive program from failure due to the vicissitudes of the market. Table 1.1 gives an example of the variations in sales from a recycling program. Specifically, the table shows the percentages by month of the yearly total shipped for major recycled materials in a regional program in New Hampshire. The shipments were from various municipalities, which are part of the New Hampshire Resource Recovery Association Cooperative Marketing Program. Comparing different materials shows that the month-by-month variation is quite substantial and illustrates how the markets for these materials are quite unrelated.

Chapter 3 presents in detail the alternative technologies available for the various steps in a recycling program. To study recycling as a production process is very helpful in obtaining a comprehensive picture and therefore is an important part of the planning process.

The emphasis in Chapter 3 is on materials that are sorted primarily by hand, since the manufacturers of assembly line separating facilities (*mixed waste processors* and *material recovery facilities*) can provide a great deal of information on their particular and specialized hardware. The chapter starts with the various methods of separation and proceeds through the steps by which these separated materials can be converted into a marketable form. This chapter makes the point that processing and storage are often crucial for selling materials at the dock (without hauling them to central facilities). The ability to sell (or even give away) at the dock greatly enhances the fiscal case for recycling programs. This discussion includes the appropriate role for capital and labor and how they can be organized. Specific examples of capital equipment include balers, granulators, glass crushers, and so on, as well as appropriate material handling equipment, structures, accumulation bins, and separation monitoring arrangements.

Chapter 4 is perhaps the most important chapter in the book, as it provides the analytical underpinnings for justifying the recycling of each material that meets the cost-benefit test. This type of analysis allows the establishment of priorities for adding goods to a recycling program based on ease of collection, high value when sold, high cost-avoidance value, and so on. Aluminum cans, glass, and corrugated cardboard are materials likely to be desirable for recycling for very different reasons. Aluminum cans, for example, are often the first thing recycled because of the high market value of aluminum. Glass bottles, on the other hand, are a low value item but represent 10 percent of the weight in the waste stream; each ton removed from the waste stream saves the town whatever it costs to get rid of a ton of glass as trash ($50 to $100 is becoming common). Corrugated paper (cardboard) is difficult to compact, so trash containers with large amounts of it must be emptied frequently. This process often involves costly haulage. Avoiding haulage costs is, therefore, a substantial gain from separating and baling cardboard. Chapter 4 is important for preparing a case for recycling. It should be noted that a number of numerical examples are provided in Chapter 4 to assist in calculating the costs and benefits.

Part II, Setting Up and Evaluating a Recycling Plan, focuses on applying the techniques and analysis from Part I. An important step early in the process of setting up a solid waste plan is presenting forceful arguments for the necessity of recycling to those who need to be convinced. As an active participant in numerous symposia, workshops, and various other public meetings, the author continues to be impressed that audiences continue to ask the same small number of questions about major issues. Examples include "When everyone recycles, won't there be a glut on the market?" "What is the point of saving newspapers when we can't get any money for them?" and "How do we get people to participate?" Chapter 5 equips individuals working on the recycling plan with answers to what the author has found to be the most common concerns.

Chapter 6 takes the techniques developed in the previous chapters and shows how they can be used to project the impact of a recycling program on solid waste disposal costs. The same material-by-material evaluation introduced in Chapter 4 is used on the total number of tons of each material, including the capability of making different assumptions about recycling rates, alternative processing, market prices, trash disposal costs, and so on. The material presented can be integrated into current and proposed budgets for a thorough, yet understandable, fiscal comparison of alternative strategies for solid waste disposal.

Chapter 7 is a crucial step as part of a long-term commitment to recycling. For obvious reasons, most programs will start with recycling a fairly limited number of items, and add more as time passes. It is therefore very likely that requests will be made to townspeople, the city council, the college president, the environmental manager, and various other decision makers for additional funding to expand the recycling effort. By far the easiest way to secure this funding is to evaluate the first stage of the program and show how it achieved the fiscal and environmental goals originally established. The techniques described in Chapters 2 to 4 can be used to sell subsequent additions to the recycling program.

Part III, Additional Perspectives on Recycling, provides for serious students of solid waste management, or any other reader, a higher level of analysis of recycling, as well as some further thoughts on the role of recycling in the global economy.

A rudimentary understanding of how some principles and concepts of economics can be applied to recycling is quite helpful, both to those planning to use this text to organize and/or evaluate recycling programs and to those simply wanting a fuller understanding of how recycling fits into the overall issue of solid waste disposal. Chapter 8 provides such an understanding. Recycling programs can be understood and sold much more successfully if the proponents have a clear sense of the analysis that often shows that such programs are cost-effective. The material in this chapter is drawn from that used in an introductory college course in microeconomics and includes such concepts as *public good, economies of scale*, and *supply and demand*. The chapter could also be used by economics instructors seeking examples in applied economics.

Chapter 9 puts recycling into a more global context. It is pointed out, for example, how solutions to the solid waste crisis are almost always presented only as a choice between landfilling and incineration (or perhaps large-scale composting). Then, recycling is discussed as a secondary consideration in terms of its impact on the flow of solid waste. At best it is discussed as a complement to one of the primary disposal methods. This chapter argues that recycling and incineration are actually substitutes for one another and that the concept of integrated waste management is fundamentally unsound.

As a number of progressive environmental thinkers have pointed out, recycling ought to be just one element of a three-prong approach to environmentally friendly solid waste management. Known as the 3Rs, this approach envisions a more comprehensive view of solid waste management, including source *reduction, reuse*, and *recycling*. Source reduction, for example, is in many ways a more advanced idea than recycling. If we could reduce the excess packaging of consumer goods and make the remaining packaging either returnable or at least easy to recycle, we would be reducing the amount of solid waste at the source. The bottle bills in effect in many states and various actual or proposed bans on disposable diapers, juice boxes, bimetal cans, and waxed milk cartons all are examples of source reduction. Recycling and source reduction are not substitutes for each other; they are complementary. If we could reduce solid waste at the source and make the remaining materials easier to recycle, there would be even less need for incineration and landfilling after recycling.

The final topic, the throw-away society, uses the notion of "think globally, act locally" to suggest how local recycling programs can catalyze efforts to make larger systemic changes in how society views the use of its scarce resources.

COMPOSTING, MANDATORY RECYCLING, AND HAZARDOUS WASTES

It is important to make clear the relationship between recycling and a related concept, *composting.* Composting, or the controlled decomposition of organic materials, on a modest scale can be an integral part of a recycling program. On a large scale, which would include the 40 percent of the waste stream which is paper, composting often is presented as a substitute for landfilling/incineration. Its application at this scale represents a new and somewhat controversial technology. For this reason, and because the author views large-scale composting as primarily a costly alternative to recycling (see Chapter 9), it is not discussed in detail herein. St. Cloud, Minnesota, has such a facility, and Keene, New Hampshire, is considering one. Appendix 2.2 provides a flow chart of a large-scale composting facility. Composting of food and yard waste on a smaller scale is considered in depth in this book as an integral part of a recycling program.

One issue often discussed is whether recycling ought to be mandatory. The view presented here is that it ought to be mandatory. Whether we are talking about an office building, shopping mall, a college or university, or a municipality, individuals should be required to separate trash for recycling whenever it pays to do so. There are several reasons for this, not the least of which is that a higher recycling rate will mean a lower cost of trash disposal. An additional justification for mandatory separation is provided by the economic theory of the public good. Public goods are things like highways, clean air, public parks, and so forth. Among the characteristics of these goods is that once provided, the gains go to everyone. Consequently, some people would try to duck payments because the goods would be available to them anyway if other people pay to provide it, (called *the free rider problem* in economics). This is why people are required by law to pay taxes to cover the cost of national defense, fire protection, public parks, highways, and a host of other things. If payment were not required, we would have far less than the appropriate amount of such goods. In the absence of mandatory separation for recycling, therefore, we would have far less to recycle than would be cost-justified. In the extreme case, some people would get all the benefits of recycling at no cost if everyone else separated while they chose not to. Making separation mandatory is simply an extension of the laws requiring individuals to send their trash to a local incinerator or landfill instead of throwing it over the back fence. In larger cities, where mandatory separation is more difficult to enforce (although still desirable), recycling programs can be backed up by automated systems that use hand labor, screens, magnets, and other means to extract recyclables from unsorted solid waste.

A significant solid waste disposal problem involves hazardous waste, which in addition to obvious residues, like toxic industrial chemicals, asbestos, and radioactive materials, includes many household products. The most onerous household waste products are worn-out batteries, but this category includes cleaning supplies, agricultural chemicals, woodworking materials, and automotive liquids. The disposal of such materials ought not to be done at conventional landfills and incinerators and is commonly handled by firms that specialize in their treatment. With a few exceptions (waste oil, for example), hazardous materials should not be handled at local recycling centers. Chapter 2 contains a complete listing of hazardous household waste, but this book does not cover the highly specialized topic of recycling hazardous waste.

PART I

Research and
Planning for Recycling

The Anatomy of a Solid Waste Stream

Solid waste is commonly described as a *stream* of discarded materials. This analogy may be a bit upsetting to some, who see solid waste as being about as different from a mountain stream as is possible. At the practical level, however, to view solid waste in this way is both helpful and realistic. Just like a flowing stream of water, food, paper, and plastic waste, as well as thousands of other items, are constantly on the move. A stream of water ultimately flows into rivers, lakes, and oceans. Solid waste ultimately flows on, in, or above the earth for disposal. The purpose here is to show how recycling can greatly reduce the size of this stream as it flows into disposal. The first step in learning about recycling is to identify all the materials available for potential recycling. For this one must learn something about the anatomy of the local waste stream.

Although calling solid waste a stream can be very helpful, it can also lead to erroneous conclusions if one is not careful. A stream of water (even a polluted one) is mostly water. Streams of solid waste, on the other hand, usually are made up of at least several very different materials and sometimes many more. Only a clear understanding of the diversity of materials in a waste stream can lead to the most effective solution for their disposal. Once this diversity is understood and appreciated, recycling often is the first choice for dealing with the problem. There is even an advantage to having a great diversity of materials in solid waste. A comprehensive recycling program involving six or eight or ten different materials will be protected from market price fluctuations in the same way that diversity reduces market risk in an investment portfolio. This point was made with Table 1.1.

The solid waste generated for every individual in the United States is close to 1 ton per year. This ton shows up in many different ways — it could

Table 2.1
Weight of Materials Discarded in Municipal Solid Waste, 1988

Aluminum	1.1%
Ferrous metals	7.0%
Food wastes	8.5%
Glass	7.1%
Other	3.4%
Paper and paperboard	34.2%
Plastics	9.2%
Rubber and leather	2.9%
Textiles	2.5%
Wood	4.2%
Yard wastes	19.9%
Total:	100.0%

Source: National Soft Drink Association, "Things You've Always Wanted to Know," 1990, p. 6.

be cardboard in a shopping mall, diapers from a hospital, scrap paper from the office building, or mixed trash from households. Although there are thousands of different waste disposal situations, it is useful to start by looking at the official breakdown of municipal solid waste in the United States. This is the anatomy of the waste stream that cities and towns deal with. The overall types and percentages by weight in municipal solid waste are given in Table 2.1. For purposes of recycling, it often pays to break each material from Table 2.1 into finer categories. For example, *paper* could be newspaper, mixed paper, corrugated paper, computer paper, white paper, and so on. Plastic is now described by the types of resin used and coded with numbers from one to seven to help identify these resins in order to determine a plastic item's recyclability.

In a typical municipal solid waste stream these percentages may be good estimates. But for shopping malls, hospitals, office buildings, schools and colleges, hotels, or restaurants, the specific makeup may be quite different. Office buildings are likely to have a large proportion of (valuable) white paper, shopping malls end up with significant amounts of cardboard, and city parks generate barrels and barrels of beverage containers. Whatever the mix in specific waste disposal situations, the first step in setting up a recycling plan is to look carefully at the anatomy of the waste stream: one must carefully determine the amount of each major waste material and how and at what cost it is being disposed of.

Analyzing the waste stream in terms of percentages is not necessarily the only helpful way to divide it up. After all, since it has to be collected, monitored, handled, and so forth, other characteristics may be important. For example, the materials could be looked at based on (1) bulkiness in storage or handling, (2) hazards in storage or handling, (3) ease of recycling, or (4) potential for repair or reuse. At the practical level, several categories often are helpful in understanding a waste stream. Consequently, thinking about a waste stream from each perspective will assist in setting up a well thought-out solid waste management program based on recycling.

PERSPECTIVES ON THE MAKEUP OF THE SOLID WASTE STREAM

Bulkiness of Materials in Handling and Storage

The waste materials discarded by households, businesses, and institutions must be handled and often stored (at least temporarily) in the process. Considerable variation exists in the bulkiness of this waste, and the cost of dealing with the bulk problem may determine whether something is worth recycling. Two items with the same value may actually be quite different when processing or storage costs are considered. A dumpster full of broken items from a furniture store, for example, contains a great deal of unused storage volume. That same dumpster filled with scrap paper from the nearby computer store will fill almost every cubic inch. Scrap metal comes in many different shapes and sizes and often is very heavy and/or awkward to handle. Old refrigerators from an apartment building renovation have quite a different value than the copper or brass fixtures from the same renovation. Corrugated cardboard is bulky to handle and store, and plastic milk jugs end up all over the ground if more than a few are hand-carried at a time.

It is the bulkiness of waste materials in the collection process that is of interest here. In other words, the concern is for bulk handling problems as the waste is gathered at the waste site, transported to a transfer area, and/or stored prior to processing. Large, awkward items or materials often produce unique problems for recycling programs; it may be useful to identify them and have them separated out for special consideration. This special treatment may occur at curbside, in the parking lot dumpster, at the back of the warehouse, or at a recycling center.

Although bulkiness is a much more subjective breakdown than percentage by weight, it is sometimes helpful to categorize waste materials by bulk. Of particular concern is the extent to which bulkiness interfers with the smooth flow of recyclables. A variety of materials are divided into three catagories according to bulk:

Very Bulky to Handle and Store: Junk furniture, scrap iron, tires,* wood and brush, appliances,* heavy demolition waste.

Moderately Bulky: Yard waste, car batteries and fluids,* plastic containers, light demolition waste, corrugated paper, nonferrous scrap.

Bulk Unlikely to Be a Problem: Aluminum and tin cans, all paper not corrugated, glass, other plastic, food waste.

*also may present hazardous waste problems

It is not surprising that one sees the items in the first category placed off to the side (in the hope they will go away) at many recycling facilities. Some materials in the second catagory may also present bulk problems at the recycling facility. This breakdown based on bulk may be very helpful to those trying to start a recycling program as part of overall solid waste management.

Bulky waste materials such as those in the first group often are examples of why recycling won't work. People say "What will you do with tires?" "Appliances are a big problem for recycling centers" and "How about that demolition waste when we tear down the old shop?" It is crucial to bear in mind that these items, and most others in the bulky category, cannot be dealt with by other solid waste disposal options, either. Appliances, junk furniture, and tires generally cannot be incinerated, landfilled, or composted. Although they represent serious waste disposal problems, these problems are unrelated to recycling as a first choice and should not be allowed to obscure the gains.

The breakdown by bulk does not necessarily mean that the very bulky items will be the most difficult to recycle. The purpose of this exercise is simply to point out that there may be considerations other than percentage in the waste stream that influence recyclability. For example, brush and (clean) wood can be quite awkward to handle, but can be chipped, stored uncovered, and require no further processing until they break down and can be sold as compost. Certain types of paper, on the other hand, may be very easy to handle during collection and storage, but a jurisdiction still may have to pay someone to take them away after separation and processing. Of course, paper may still be a good deal for recycling, considering the cost of disposing of it as trash. In other words, bulkiness must be considered and then factored in as appropriate in planning for recycling.

Hazards in Handling, Transportation, or Storage

When the term *hazardous waste* is mentioned, we probably think first of those things that have gotten the most adverse (and often tragic) publicity in recent years—dioxin, DDT, and radioactive waste come to mind. The problems related to these materials are well documented. They also tend to be concentrated in certain industrial processes and specialized sites, which makes them somewhat easier to control (DDT was an exception). There continue to be, however, other widely distributed hazardous materials. These often present unique disposal problems for thousands of solid waste disposal managers. Among the better known of these are polychlorinated biphenyls (PCBs) (found in the electrical system of many appliances), asbestos, and lead. The latter two are commonly found in building renovation waste. The insulation and shingles may be of asbestos, and the paint scrapings and pipe may contain lead. The extent of disposal problems with hazardous waste does not stop here, however. The list of commonly available hazardous

Table 2.2
Percentage of Household Hazardous Waste by General Type

Household Maintenance Items (mostly paint-related)	36.6%
Household Batteries	18.6%
Personal Care Products	12.1%
Cleaners	11.5%
Automotive-Maintenance Products	10.5%
Pesticides, plus pet supplies, and fertilizers	4.1%
Hobby/Other	3.4%
Pharmaceuticals	3.2%

Source: "Household Hazardous Waste," University of Arizona, Garbage Project, 1988.

materials found in households, maintenance sheds, paint shops, farm sheds, and many other commercial and institutional sites runs to the hundreds. Sooner or later most of these materials enter the waste flow and must be disposed of.

Although some communities, institutions, and firms are dealing with these wastes through specialized hazardous waste disposal companies, many become part of the regular stream of waste. Therefore, even a well-run recycling center/transfer station, or other disposal or waste storage site, can be a hazardous place to work. This is in addition to the normal physical and mental hazards involved in dealing with machinery and materials that are often dirty, heavy, and jagged. The well-known Garbage Project at the University of Arizona has estimated the proportion of the various types of hazardous waste likely to show up in the regular waste stream. Although these are called *household hazardous waste*, they are found in many sites other than households. For instance, cleaners, paints, landscaping materials, and motorized vehicles are found in most places where people live, work, or shop. The overall percentages of the various products, as estimated by the Garbage Project, are shown in Table 2.2.

These products represent an acute problem within the larger general problem of waste disposal. This is true whether we are talking about hazards to individuals employed in working with solid waste or the negative effects of inappropriate disposal on the health and safety of residents in general.

Many different means exist for dealing with hazardous waste. Tires are generally separated from the waste stream and removed for what is often a large fee, waste oil can be reused in special furnaces or refined, and car batteries can often be sold for internal materials recovery. Increasingly communities have been designating certain days for household hazardous waste drop-off and have hired specialized waste dealers to accept this waste at a very high cost. To alert solid waste disposal managers to all the potential hazards in the regular waste stream, it seems appropriate to give a more detailed listing of problematic materials. The items listed here have been identified as hazardous by a typical processor of hazardous household waste.

From the Garage

Antifreeze
Brake fluid
Wax polish
Engine degreaser
Carburetor cleaner
Creosote
Radiator flushes
Asphalt
Roofing tar
Air conditioner refrigerants
Car batteries (to be recycled)

From the House

Drain cleaners
Oven cleaners
Furniture polish
Metal polish
Window cleaners
Expired prescriptions
Arts and crafts supplies
Photography chemicals
Floor cleaners
Chemistry kits
Mothballs
Rug and upholstery cleaners

From the Workbench

Rust preventatives
Wood preservatives
Wood strippers
Wood stains
Paint thinner
Oil-based paint
Solvents
Degreasers
Sealants
Varnish

From the Yard

Pesticides (including DDT and chlordane)
Herbicides
Insect sprays
Rodent killers
Pool chemicals
No-Pest strips
Fertilizers
Cesspool cleaners
Silvex, Weed-B-Gone,
Penta Wood Preservative

Source: Keene, N.H., 1990, Ashuelot Valley Refuse District.

These materials may show up in many different situations. Wherever they appear in the waste stream, they may affect the health and safety of waste management employees far in excess of their weight or volume. They also present serious storage, handling, and disposal problems. Consideration of the hazards of such materials must take a very high priority in any solid waste planning program.

Ease of Recycling

Any recycling program should be started with those items that require the least amount of overall handling, storage, and processing per dollar gained. It must be emphasized that the major gain for some materials is from sale and for other materials it is from not having to pay to dispose of them as trash (costs avoided). Hence, materials may be prime candidates for recycling for either reason.

Although such listings are somewhat arbitrary, items can be classified according to ease of recycling:

Significant Gains from Modest Effort: Aluminum cans, yard waste, nonferrous scrap metal, reusable items (books, toys, used clothing, etc.)

Some Gains from Modest Effort: Most types of paper, glass, many plastics,* tin, scrap iron, food waste, brush

Considerable Difficulty: Certain plastics (multiresin containers), bimetal cans, tires, appliances, junk furniture, demolition waste

*Although HDPE and PET are most widely recycled, solid waste made up of the other common resins (LDPE, PP, PS, and PVC) can also be recycled and should be considered. The complete names of these resins appear in Table 2.3.

At the practical level, it is sometimes necessary to start a recycling program with something that gives a clear-cut return to the residents, employees, students, or whomever so that they see that recycling is a good idea. The list here suggests certain items that could be the first recycled. Aluminum cans and nonferrous metals are obvious candidates because of their market value. Yard waste and reusable items can also be incorporated early on if residents understand the concept of avoidance cost. In any case, ease of recycling is a useful criterion in starting up a recycling program.

Potential for Substitution, Repair, or Reuse

The term *recycling* is usually taken to mean that the separated item is broken down in some way and reprocessed to be used again as a raw material. Recent interest has focused on more direct methods of reducing the waste stream. Among these are substitution, repair, and reuse. *Substitution* usually means to replace a throw-away item with a more permanent one (cloth grocery bags instead of paper ones, for example). *Repair* means to convert broken items into usable ones (Toys for Tots programs are examples of this), and *reuse* means to either find a different use for an item or find someone for whom it still has value (used or obsolete office machinery or furniture are examples). Each example shows how the waste stream can be reduced without worrying about the processing or marketing necessary in a recycling program. A number of solid waste action groups have been presenting recycling as the option after these other possibilities have been exhausted. Although these activities may involve minor expenditures of time, labor, or resources, programs to encourage substitution, repair, or reuse can be very cost-effective. The list that follows provides examples of substitution and reuse (*repair* is self-explanatory).

Examples of Substitution

- Purchase and use of permanent shopping bags
- Running a contest to reward employees (or students) who think up substitutions that reduce disposal costs
- Buying materials in relatively large quantities to reduce packaging per pound
- Buying materials from loose stocks to minimize prepackaging
- Buying products that advertise minimum packaging
- Avoiding "disposable" products

Examples of Reuse

- Saving, and using repeatedly, cardboard boxes, buckets, pallets, and other types of stout containers
- Saving packing materials for reuse. Such items, if made of plastic, have a very long life.
- Saving and reusing all kinds of envelopes
- Announcing in a company, hospital, or school newsletter, that all furniture, office machinery, and so on no longer needed in one particular place is available for reuse.
- Carefully sorting through used clothing, toys, books, and household items for those which can be donated to clothing charities, used to stock swap shops at recycling centers, or can be sold at tag sales and flea markets.

FURTHER BREAKDOWN OF SIGNIFICANT WASTE MATERIALS

In an early section of this chapter the solid waste stream was broken down by percentages of its major constituents — paper, plastic, glass, and so forth. This diversity of materials was noted as an important ingredient in the success of a recycling program because of its ability to reduce market risk. At the practical level a breakdown of materials into the specific types of paper, glass, plastic, and so on is necessary because it is for these more exact categories that the actual markets exist.

Paper

The percentage of any material in the waste stream, and the breakdown of this material into its significant subtypes, can only be estimated at best. It varies by region, by time of year, from year to year, and in any case is difficult to count. It is generally agreed that the category of paper (about 40 percent of the waste stream) is made up of roughly 25 percent newspaper, 25 percent corrugated, and 50 percent mixed types.

Newspaper and corrugated paper are fairly standard items, although recyclers must deal with such issues as minimum thickness standards for corrugated and the percentage of magazines allowed with newspaper. Mixed paper, on the other hand, contains many different types of paper, some moderately valuable in the market and some of negative value. Even the term *mixed paper* has different meanings. As used here, it means anything that is primarily paper and is neither newspaper nor corrugated. Other paper classification systems, such as that listed next (for the recycling program of the state government of New Hampshire), has mixed paper as a subcategory in a classification system based on the ease of recycling rather than on an all-inclusive list. Note that in this system, newspaper is classified as mixed paper and cardboard and magazines are (mis)classified as nonrecyclable.

White Ledger Paper	Mixed Paper	Non-Recyclable
All white office paper	Colored paper	Glossy paper
Bright white computer paper	Newspaper*	Carbon paper
Carbon copies (w/o carbon)	Envelopes (windowless)	Waxed paper
	Flat white computer paper	Greasy paper
Typing paper	Manila folders	Soiled paper
White tablet sheets (w/o backing)	Carbonless paper	Napkins
	Cover stock (colored)	Paper towels
Adding machine tape		Paper plates
Mimeo paper		Cardboard*
Photocopy paper		Chipboard
Cover stock		Photographic paper
		Blue print paper
		Plasticized paper
		Rubber bands
		Styrofoam
		Magazines*
		Shredded paper
		Envelopes with windows
		Post-it pads
		Books

*Commonly recycled alone when processing is available

Source: New Hampshire, Governor's Recycling Program, Interdepartmental Communication, July 25, 1989.

There are many other definitions of mixed paper. For example, some manufacturers of Sono Tubes, forms for circular concrete pillars, define mixed paper as almost any kind of paper and will accept it as the basic raw material for that product. In other instances, mixed paper is only glossy

Table 2.3
Percentage of Plastics by Type of Resin Used

	Plastics (% by weight of all plastics)	Code (On bottom of container)
Low density polyethylene (LDPE)	41%	4
High density polyethylene (HDPE)	29%	2
Polypropylene (PP)	10%	5
Polystyrene (PS)	9%	6
Polyethylene terephthalate (PET)	6.5%	1
Polyvinylchloride (PVC)	4%	3
Miscellaneous (usually mixed)	0.5%	7

Source: Society of the Plastics Industry, *Plastics World,* September 1989, p. 13.
See Table 2.4

paper, including magazines, catalogues, and newspaper inserts. Newspaper itself can be of several categories. Super News is newspaper from which all glossy inserts have been removed, while #1 News contains small amounts of such contaminants. Newspaper containing significant percentages of glossy material would probably be recycled in the mixed paper category. Examples of signs for white and mixed paper programs on a college campus are given in Appendixes 2.1A and 2.1B.

Two crucial considerations should be part of a mixed paper recycling program: (1) determining what the buyers want and selecting the buyer with the most inclusive definitions, and (2) making sure that the buyer's definition of mixed paper is not going to change. Once the residents, office workers, custodial personnel, students, and others become accustomed to a certain definition of mixed paper, they will not deal well with changes, and individuals at the processing end will have to do a lot of separating.

Of course local recyclers often adjust their definitions of what is marketable. Cardboard, for example, which is listed by New Hampshire as non-recyclable, can be sold in baled form and offers significant cost-avoidance gains to towns, shopping malls, warehouses, and office buildings.

Plastics

Plastics usually are identified according to the type of resin in the product. Estimates of the percentage of plastics in the solid waste stream by weight

Table 2.4
Uses of Plastics by Type of Resin, before and after Recycling

	Typical Uses	Potential Uses after Recycling
LDPE:	plastic bags and food wrap	non-structural plastic lumber, trash cans
HDPE:	plastic "bottles" for milk, detergents, oil, low voltage wire insulation, automobile gas tanks	non-structural plastic lumber, trash cans, restroom partitions, shower cubicles, vanities, locker room benches
PP:	automobile parts, food storage containers, "cello" wrap, industrial carpet	auto parts
PS:	foam containers, packing beads, clear "glassware," cassettes, blister (stiff) packaging	foam insulation board for houses and roadbeds.
PET:*	carbonated beverage bottles, Dacron,^{tm} Mylar,^{tm} audio and video tape	soda bottles, fiber insulation for clothing
PVC:	water and drain pipe, clear flexible bottles, house siding, leather substitute, vinyl floor covering, wire and cable	

*The S.P.I. code is PETE; the plastics industry acronym is PET.

average out at 7 or 8 percent, but it may be as much as a very visible 20 percent by volume. In recent years the plastics industry has been identified as one of the worst offenders of the throw-away society. In response to this bad press, the Society of the Plastics Industry, the industry trade group, has moved to promote recycling. Foremost among its efforts has been establishing a coding system to identify the resin used in most plastic containers. This helps a great deal in separation for recycling. Table 2.3 shows the percentage breakdown according to the resin in the plastic material.

The primary uses of these plastics, and the potential uses when recycled, are shown by type of resin in Table 2.4.

Recycling rates for plastics have historically been very low when compared to aluminum, paper, and glass. There are several reasons for this, but one of the most important is the very low value/volume ratio for plastic. This means that transportation costs will overwhelm any potential gain from resale of separated material. In addition, the plastics industry has only recently shown interest in reusing recycled material. The recent development of processing equipment to densify waste plastic by shredding, granulating, or baling makes recycling of plastic much more attractive. It greatly increases the value/volume ratio, making transportation less of a limiting factor in plastics recycling. Densified plastics still require substantial storage, however, since plastics recyclers usually purchase only large loads on site. Outdoor storage after processing does offer a potentially low cost solution to the plastics storage problem.

Glass

Glass bottles represent somewhat less than 10 percent of the solid waste stream. The three standard types of glass are clear, green, and brown, with clear generally having the highest value and brown the lowest. Although the market price of separated glass is usually quite low, the very high density of glass, even uncrushed, makes it a material for which costs avoided can be substantial. It is also unburnable bulk in an incinerator and hence undesirable for disposal in that way.

Since the market value is quite low, it is necessary to prepare glass for sale through crushing, separation by color, and accumulation to substantial amounts (perhaps 20 tons of one color). It must also be carefully monitored to avoid contamination. It should be noted that glass can also be used as a roadbed base in "glassphalt" and as landfill cover. For these purposes separation by color is usually not necessary.

Care must be used when handling glass because of the harm it can do to recycling attendants and the tires of machinery. It is not recommended that clients at the recycling center crush or smash their own glass bottles. Inexpensive commercial glass crushers are available.

Aluminum Cans and Other Aluminum

The solid waste stream contains about 2 percent aluminum, although this figure is probably rising slowly. Aluminum beverage containers, which constitute about half the total amount of aluminum, are unique in that it pays to recycle them under almost any circumstances. They are easy to separate, easy to handle, are rarely contaminated, are made from a single material, and have a high market value. Transportation costs per pound-mile are reduced by compaction, but it is rarely necessary for recycling them. Aluminum beverage containers are frequently the first item chosen for a new recycling program.

Other types of aluminum can also be recycled. Chair frames, aluminum cans other than beverage containers, aluminum foil, aluminum wire, as well as heavy aluminum such as engine blocks and motorcycle frames, have good potential for recycling. The buyers of "other aluminum" are often scrap metal dealers; therefore such items are likely to be part of a scrap metal separation program.

Scrap Metal

Five percent or more of the solid waste stream may be made up of various types of scrap metal. Even excluding automobiles — which do present unique problems, but are usually not considered part of the solid waste disposal responsibility of readers of this book — scrap metal is a category in which a great deal of variation is found in its recyclability. At one extreme is scrap copper, which may bring close to $1.00 per pound; at the other extreme are appliances (often called *white goods*), which in recent years have become at best a break-even proposition for recycling. Although different scrap buyers may have different categories of metals, the listing in Table 2.5 from the New Hampshire Department of Environmental Services gives an idea of the variation that exists even within several of the better-defined categories. These categories are only representative; a more complete listing would include several types of light iron, other categories of aluminum, and a number of other nonferrous metals (copper, brass, lead, etc.).

Yard Waste

The brush, twigs, leaves, and grass clippings that can make up at least 15 percent of the waste stream, is called *yard waste*. The term *yard* in *yard waste* seems to imply that it comes only from residences, but this is not the case. Many businesses and institutions, as well as various types of parks, generate large amounts of these materials. Many people in rural or suburban areas take the simple route and deal with yard waste (and also garden and food waste) with a home compost pile. However, the majority of yard waste does show up at landfills and incinerators. Together with aluminum beverage containers, yard waste is an item easily incorporated in the initial stages of a recycling program. The ease of recycling is different than with aluminum because yard waste can be dumped on the ground, uncovered, in any uncontaminated spot. Nothing has to be done to it (unless food waste is included — discussed next), and in a couple of years, starting from the first loads dumped, it can be sold by the bagful for all kinds of agricultural and landscape uses. Larger brush and wood can be incorporated if a chipper is used, and clean wood ash can be added to improve the quality. Various mechanical means can be used to speed up the composting process. See Appendix 2.3 for a detailed discussion of composting possibilities for food and yard waste and possibly sewage sludge.

Table 2.5
Scrap Metal Breakdown by Common Products and Materials

White Goods/Appliances	Aluminum/No Wood Attached
Air Conditioners	Cast Aluminum Engine Blocks
Washing Machines and Dryers	Cloths Drying Racks
Dishwashers	House Siding
Fans	Lawn Chairs w/o Webbing
Freezers	Mailboxes, no Wood or Concrete
Hot Water Tanks	Pots and Pans
Irons	Ducts from Heating Systems
Ovens	Screen Frames
Refrigerators	Siding from Mobile Homes
Stoves and Stove Hoods	Ski Poles
Toasters	Snow Shovels
Trash Compactors	Storm Windows/Doors
Typewriters	Television Antennas
	Tent Poles
Cast Iron	**Heavy Unshreddable Iron**
Ax/Sledge Hammer Heads	Heavy Pipe
Car Axles	Heavy Storage Tanks
Cast Iron Cookware	Structural Steel
Ferrous Engine Blocks	Wheel Rims
Hibachi Grills	Brake Drums
Radiators	
Sinks and Tubs	
Sewer Pipes	
Tool Sheds	
Truck Caps, no Fiberglass	

Source: New Hampshire, Department of Environmental Services, "Technical Bulletin No. 13," 1990.

Food Waste

Food waste, about 15 percent of the waste stream, is a highly degradable organic material. It presents problems, however, for both incinerators (too much moisture) and landfills (noxious odors and the attraction of unwanted creatures). It can be incorporated in a recycling program, but presents some public relations problems in separation. Most people are used to the convenience and aesthetic advantage of diluting food waste by mixing it with paper and other household trash or putting it down a garbage disposal (where it becomes a different disposal problem).

It can be recycled in at least two ways, either as feed for certain farm animals or as part of a municipal composting plan. Recycling programs that choose composting, a potentially much larger use than animal feed, must carefully investigate the techniques available. If food waste is incorporated with yard waste, care must be taken to prevent odors and problems with rodents. If paper is added, problems with contamination and incomplete decomposition can occur. In the case of composting programs that include paper and yard and food waste, professional assistance must be sought and considerable capital expenditure may be required.

Reusable Items

By some estimates, up to 10 percent or more of the solid waste stream is made up of items that could be reused fairly easily. Obvious examples are clothing, books, toys, and furniture. As discussed earlier, many recycling centers have some type of swap shop to store and distribute such items. Another possibility would be to have local social service agencies provide collection points at the recycling facility. Even if given away, the community gains in two ways — the costs of landfilling are avoided, and the individuals taking the items are getting something they value.

Tires

Tires can be up to 2 percent of the waste stream, generally are not landfilled, and cannot be burned adequately in a conventional incinerator. They also present a serious fire hazard as recent experiences in California and New Hampshire have shown. Research is being done on using them for oil recovery, as a binder in asphalt, and in the manufacture of rubber products. Among current uses are as dynamite blankets, for swinging and climbing at school playgrounds, and as fuel in special tire-burning waste-to-energy plants. An example of the latter is an operating 14-megawatt plant built by Oxford Energy in Modesto, California. This is the only such plant operating in the United States, but Oxford is nearing completion of an additional plant in Sterling, Connecticut, and has plans for three more. The Connecticut plant

Table 2.6
The Recyclability of Household Batteries

Category	Hazard	Recyclable in U.S.A.	Description and Use
PRIMARY			
(discharged once and discarded)			
- zinc carbon	Mercury	No	general purpose
- alkaline manganese	Mercury	No	toys, flashlights, smoke alarms
- button cells			
lithium	Lithium	No	hearing aids
mercuric oxide	Mercury	Yes	calculators
silver oxide	Silver, Mercury	Yes	watches, cameras
zinc air	Mercury	No	medical devices
SECONDARY			
(rechargeable)			
- nickel cadmium	Cadmium	Yes	rechargeable tools, appliances, and general use

Source: New Hampshire, Department of Environmental Services, "Technical Bulletin," 1990, p. 4.

will burn twelve to thirteen million tires annually and produce 30 megawatts of energy (enough for 30,000 households). The tipping fee at the Connecticut plant is about forty cents per tire, with a somewhat lower fee in California (Phillips, 1991, p. 50).

Tin Cans

Tin is a relatively small portion of the solid waste stream, about 1 percent, but the tin industry seems to be increasingly concerned that it is losing out to recycling initiatives taken by other container industries. Recyclers are therefore finding for the first time that there are buyers (or at least removers)

Table 2.7
Construction and Demolition Generation and Reuse in Vermont (1989)

	Generation	Reuse Recycling Tons/Year
Asphalt	225,000	112,500
	(46%)*	(50%)
Concrete	70,000	14,000
	(14%)	(20%)
Metal	25,000	10,000
	(5%)	(40%)
Wood	125,000	62,5000
	(26%)	(50%)
Other		
Mixed C & D	45,000	3,250
	(9%)	(7%)
Total	490,000	202,250
	(100%)	(41%)**

Source: Robert Spencer, "Taking Control of C&D Debris," *Biocycle*, July 1991, p. 65.
*Percentage of all construction and demolition materials.
**Percentage of all construction and demolition materials recycled.

for tin, and it should be considered for a recycling program. It is interesting to note that although tin is only a very small percentage of the weight of a "tin can" (up to 4 percent), it represents up to one-third of the can's value.

Miscellaneous

Different institutional settings generate different types of miscellaneous waste. Municipal solid waste, for example, contains 4.2 percent wood, 2.9 percent rubber and leather, and 2.5 percent textiles. A major disposal problem wherever materials are unpacked from shipping, say in a shopping mall, is styrofoam beads. In hospitals it is medical waste and diapers. Colleges and universities are stuck with junk furniture at the end of the year. The telephone company has hundreds of wooden wire spools to get rid of. In the process of identifying the ingredients in their waste streams, disposal managers must appreciate that they may discover unique problems requiring unique solutions. A good example of a unique recycling problem is that related to the disposal of household batteries. Although batteries are a major source of toxic materials in landfills, Table 2.6 shows that certain types can be recycled.

Another difficult waste disposal problem, and one that arises in many different situations, is how to deal with construction and demolition waste. Table 2.7 gives a typical breakdown for the generation and recycling of construction and demolition (C&D) waste. For a more detailed breakdown of C&D waste, see Appendix 2.4.

SUMMARY

Municipal solid waste disposal is but one of many different solid waste disposal situations in which recycling is helpful. In this chapter we saw that a crucial first step in knowing how to deal with a particular solid waste problem is knowing in detail what it contains. Once the various materials in a waste stream are identified, the next step is to look at the technology available to recycle them. The processes and equipment for dealing with recyclables are the subject of Chapter 3.

From Trash to Market: The Stages of a Recycling Program

Chapter 2 discussed several different ways of breaking down a solid waste stream. It also noted that a careful identification of the types and amounts of the large variety of materials in a stream of solid waste is critical in planning for recycling. This chapter looks in detail at the various systems for extracting the identified materials from the waste stream and converting them to marketable commodities.

We tend to think of materials separation as being the key to recycling. Although separation is important, a serious recycling program is much more than that. It is more accurately described as a process with a number of steps, separation being only the first. The recycling process is discussed here as a number of stages—the stages that convert the various materials so they can move from trash to market.

To be totally accurate, it should be pointed out that there are at least three fundamentally different technologies available for recycling. We will call these three technologies *tracks*; each has its own series of stages. The major difference in these technologies is in their use of machinery for separating and processing recyclables. In the first and most common, separation is done primarily by individuals at the point where the materials become waste. This we refer to as *source-specific separation* (the *SSS track*). In the second, materials are separated into recyclables and nonrecyclables at the source and then further separated by specialized equipment at a large, central facility called a *materials recovery facility* (the *MRF track*). The materials that have been taken out for recycling but are still mixed are referred to as *commingled*. Commingled recyclables are separated at the MRF, a process that

Figure 3.1
Three Solid Waste Technologies Containing Recycling

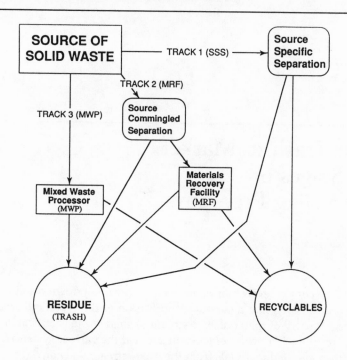

is part of the MRF track. In the third and least common process, recyclables are removed from mixed waste with specialized equipment at a central facility. This we refer to as *mixed waste processing* (the *MWP track*), as that is what these facilities are called. Figure 3.1 is a simple representation of these three tracks for extracting recyclables from the solid waste stream.

In a field in which innovation is the norm, there are always exceptions to general concepts like the three tracks. Even with this weakness, Figure 3.1 captures the important difference in these three technologies. Most of the discussion on the stages of recycling below will follow the SSS track, since variants of this are by far the most common. SSS would cover not only curbside and household sorting and drop-off residential programs but also most recycling efforts in office buildings, hospitals, college dormitories, shopping malls, schools, and many other areas where separation is done near the point at which the material becomes waste. The other two tracks will be discussed later in the chapter.

The transformation of mixed waste into marketable commodities often involves a number of the stages alluded to earlier. Using the SSS track as the model, these stages could include any or all of the following:

- Diversion, separation, or extraction. The items to be recycled must be separated or extracted from the waste stream or, better yet, diverted before becoming trash.
- Pickup and delivery. The separated materials usually must be moved or delivered to a central site for processing.
- Accumulation. Processing, or even sale without processing, usually requires temporary accumulation to required volumes or weights before processing or direct sale. For example, once a bale of cardboard is started, there must be enough cardboard on hand to make the whole bale. Using a baler to store partial bales is likely to be very inefficient.
- Processing. The successful recycling of many items involves processing to substantially increase density. The increased weight per unit of volume (i.e., density) prevents the market value of the material from being overwhelmed by storage and transportation costs. Processing may involve balers, granulators, wood chippers, glass crushers, and various other types of machinery. This should not be confused with the processing of commingled recyclables in a materials recovery facility or the processing of trash in a mixed waste processor.
- Storage. Buyers often require a minimum number of bales, or other units of processed material, to ensure pickup at the seller's dock. Storage space may therefore be a cost-effective investment.
- Transportation. The discussion of storage implies that to some extent transportation and storage are substitutes for each other. Either store enough to have the buyer come to the facility, or haul smaller amounts to the buyer's location. The economics of the situation will dictate which. It is also possible that buyers will take smaller shipments if they are delivered than if it is necessary for them to pick up.

Planning for successful recycling requires that the whole process be laid out beforehand. The stages of recycling model described in this chapter will be very helpful to this end. As each potentially recyclable material is studied in its turn, it is clear that the amount available and the market price are not all that matter. Materials may also have to go through several stages of recycling, which must be understood and taken into account. It is a prescription for failure not to research each material in the context of its path through these stages.

There are also recurring activities that may have to be attended to at several stages. Foremost among these are materials handling and three different kinds of monitoring. Recycled newspaper, plastics, glass, and so on have to be handled at each recycling stage. Once a bale of recyclables is made, for example, at least several hundred pounds of newspaper, plastic, or whatever often have to be moved from processing to storage to the back of a truck. Proper equipment for heavy materials handling therefore is crucial. Each of the following monitoring activities is important:

- monitoring the separation effort; that is, making sure that recyclables have been removed from the trash.

- monitoring each of the separated materials to make sure there is no commingling.
- monitoring the carefully separated materials to make sure there is no contamination attached or mixed in.

At each stage, monitoring has to be done to ensure a final product that is as marketable as possible. Whole loads of granulated plastic have been rejected by buyers because a very small amount of a contaminant was granulated and spread throughout the load. Aluminum cans sometimes get mixed with tin, glossies can be mixed with newspapers meant for animal bedding, and plastic bags are found inside brown grocery bags. And, of course, losses result whenever recycled materials are left in the trash. Reference to and discussion of materials handling and monitoring are made wherever appropriate. Sections on the types of monitoring appear in the discussion of the stage at which it is most commonly done. Each stage of recycling is discussed in detail here, but it should be noted that not all stages are encountered in each recycling situation.

TRACK 1 (SSS) RECYCLING

Stage 1—Diversion, Separation, Extraction

Numerous mechanisms are developed by recycling managers, staff committees, or the recycling population for removing recyclables from the waste stream. It is important that care be taken in developing these techniques so as to encourage innovation. If separation is mandatory, educational efforts could be directed toward assisting the separators, whether they are members of households, employees of various businesses, students, or whomever, in efficient ways of extracting, cleaning, and storing recyclables and in preparing the materials for pickup or drop-off. If the recycling program is not mandatory, educational efforts would be directed toward selling the population on the benefits of recycling, as well as providing guidance in specific recycling tasks. It is perhaps obvious, but important enough to be worth repeating, that any kind of recycling plan needs the cooperation of the generators of the trash. Hence care must be taken to educate for maximum ease and simplicity in the various recycling tasks individuals must undertake at or near the points where solid material becomes trash. Poorly thought-out procedures that require frequent adjustments are likely to have a very negative effect on the recycling population at the point at which their cooperation is likely to be the most necesssary.

The separation of recyclables is most often done at or near the site where they become waste. As mentioned earlier, recycling at this stage is far simpler if the materials can be diverted before becoming trash. Although stores and catalogues sell many varieties of separation bins, it is also true that people have evolved any number of creative arrangements for holding separated recyclables. In some cases there is a bin for each material at the point of diversion, extraction, or separation. A white paper container at a copy machine, a cardboard bin where stock is unpacked, and several wastebaskets in a kitchen are all good examples. In other cases, all similar recyclables are initially put together—all plastic, aluminum, and glass bottles together, all paper together, all bags together—and then are further sorted at pickup or when delivered to a processing facility (partial commingling). The use of color-coded containers is helpful, but the reuse of cardboard boxes for temporary storage is less expensive and fits in well with the philosophy of conserving materials.

There are several considerations regarding the location of containers to hold materials at the first stage of recycling. The containers should of course be clean, sturdy, and clearly marked. They should be as close to the separators as possible, while accounting for the needs of those who do the pickup. Regarding pickup, it must be remembered that each stop takes time and labor, and hence an accommodation must be found between the distance from the separators to the bins on one hand and the amount of time and resources available to the pick-up crew on the other. This is less of a problem with household separation if residents either take the material to the recycling facility or put it out for curbside pickup. Obviously, it is important to have a clear and simple description of what should be included in all deposit areas where employees, visitors, students, or other nonhousehold groups are depositing recyclables. This is particularly true for the different grades of paper, as it is difficult to separate paper after it has been commingled.

At this stage, materials handling can usually be done by hand or with hand trucks. The recyclables will be unprocessed, so they are likely to have a low density and be of only modest weight.

Separation Monitoring. At some point the separation effort should be monitored. The *separation effort* can be defined as the amount of the various materials actually separated as a proportion of the total amount initially in the waste stream. An alternative definition would be the amount recycled as a percent of the amount initially estimated. The latter concept is discussed in Chapter 7 on evaluation. The success rate (i.e., recycling percentage) could be different for different materials in the waste stream, an outcome that, incidently, might focus attention on those items with low recycling rates. *Monitoring* is a term that could be applied to either a mandatory or voluntary recycling program. For a mandatory municipal program, it can be thought of as equivalent to the local police monitoring car speed on the roads or the animal control officer checking license tags. What has to be monitored primarily is the unseparated portion of the trash because that is where the recyclables remain that should have been removed. (Note: The monitoring of the recyclable stream itself—finding tin cans mixed with aluminum cans, for example—is covered in the section on processing recyclables.) Separation monitoring can be done at any point near where the separation, diversion, or extraction takes place. The initial step is one of choosing a point in the movement of materials where monitoring is the most efficient. This could be either at the curbside on trash pick-up day, in an office or warehouse when trash pickup is done, or at a transfer station, landfill, or incinerator when trash is delivered.

Before instituting a major separation monitoring program, it makes sense to check whether such a program is necessary. Perhaps the easiest way to do this is to periodically sample the trash further down stream, say, at the accumulation point. This might not involve more than a once daily removal for cutting open and inspecting a bag from each of ten different loads. If this process generates an acceptably high recycling rate, a more intensive monitoring system may be unnecessary.

Because of the labor required, significant monitoring of the trash stream can be costly. Some types of sampling of the participants might be more appropriate; if done properly, one can get decent information at very modest cost. In general, fairness would dictate that the sampling should be random, meaning that everyone has an equal chance of being sampled. One type of sampling is *with replacement*, meaning that even if a household, work station, or dormitory floor has already had its trash looked into, it is as likely to be chosen again as those who have not been sampled. This would induce participants to maintain separation efforts even if they had just been monitored. From a public relations perspective, however, it might be preferable to instead use *without replacement*, meaning that those selected for monitoring recently will not be subject to having their names drawn for a certain amount of time. Among the many sampling variations, at least two are worthy of note. When participants fail the monitoring, it might be appropriate, in addition to other sanctions, to arrange the sampling so that their chances of being chosen are increased. Also, since the cost of inadequate separation varies directly with the amount of trash under consideration, it might be proper that the larger sources have a greater probability of being selected for monitoring. This is not random with regard to participants, but if the probabilities are in proportion to trash generated, it would be random with regard to weight of trash.

Stage 2—Pickup and Delivery

As has been noted, the separation of recyclables is most often done close to the physical site where they become either residues, no longer needed packaging, or some other type of solid waste. These materials must then be collected and transported to a specialized facility for processing and (it is hoped) sale. A number of methods exist for collection and transportation, with a common one the so-called drop-off, whereby the generator of the waste takes the separated items to a recycling or accumulation facility. Other methods are common, however, especially curbside pickup in larger towns and cities. Appendix 3.3 contains a listing of dealers specializing in curbside recycling trucks and trailers. Waste generators may also have special containers strategically located around town or in scattered locations in shopping malls, cafeterias, recreation areas, office buildings, schools, and so on. These containers are periodically picked up and taken to recycling or processing centers. Other types of intermediate storage include local sites for collection and accumulation and regional centers for processing and marketing. Care must be taken, however, to minimize the transportation of unprocessed recyclables. Items such as cardboard and plastics are costly to transport in an unprocessed state and therefore should be baled, granulated, shredded, or whatever as soon as possible after they are thrown away. With processing, they could be accumulated, stored, and sold out of a larger regional facility.

Stage 3 — Accumulation

Materials brought into a recycling center often must be accumulated before processing. This is particularly true when several different materials are processed on the same piece of equipment — cardboard, newspaper, HDPE plastic, and PET plastic on the same baler, for example. Those not being loaded on the baler must be kept somewhere until their turn comes. Bins of various types (usually wood or concrete) are normally used for temporary storage and are filled after monitoring the separated materials. A careful design will place such bins so as to minimize materials handling. The size and location (and even the necessity) of such bins will depend on the material that has been recycled. Paper that is going to be baled has to be kept from the weather and so needs to be stored in covered bins. The minimization of materials handling suggests that they be near the baler. Some materials do not need bins and can be stored on the ground outdoors. Examples of such materials include the various types of metal scrap and yard waste (and even food waste if it is part of a composting program). Because of significant materials handling problems, the bins used for glass ought to be large enough — often holding up to 20 tons of one color — to also serve as storage for processed glass. That way, it does not have to be moved again until it is picked up for sale. Small glass crushers are available that can be easily used as feeders for the glass bin and thereby allow accumulation to become storage without further handling. Other accumulation (and storage) containers include 55-gallon drums, old boxcars or trailer boxes, large community containers called igloos, and cardboard or plastic gaylords (heavy boxes about 1 cubic yard in volume).

Materials Monitoring. Contamination is a significant problem for firms that produce products using recycled materials. It could be small amounts of waxed paper in with newspaper, ceramic doodads attached to glass wine bottles, tin cans with aluminum bottoms, or any number of other problems. Contamination often reduces the value of recyclables or even makes the difference between marketability and nonmarketability. It is very important to the success of any recycling program that separated materials are scanned carefully prior to processing for sale. Since processing often involves baling, shredding, chipping, or granulating, a small amount of a missed contaminant can ruin a large volume of the recycled material.

It is strongly advised that recycling centers provide an intermediate accumulation capability between the delivery of the recyclables and their accumulation and/or processing and/or storage for sale. A series of heavy tables or long counters, with public access on one side only, provides an efficient arrangement for monitoring recyclables. Employees or trained volunteers work on the secured side of the tables and check the materials before putting them in their proper receptacles for accumulation and processing. An additional benefit of this set-up and procedure is that it keeps the public away from the various (and often dangerous) machinery associated with modern recycling centers. Of course this system also allows employees to check to make sure that each specific category of recyclables is made up only of that item. This means no tin with aluminum, no glossies with Super News, no broken windowpanes with clear glass bottles, and so forth.

The monitoring of recyclables can be made easier and cheaper by educational programs that train households, firms, and institutions so that they are alert for contaminants and use care in their own separation activities.

For any particular item being separated out for processing and resale, the definition of a *contaminant* depends on the needs of the buyers of the product; these buyers should be consulted accordingly. Of course it is always true that recycled materials should be dirt-free and cleaned of organic material.

One category of materials particularly challenging from a monitoring perspective is scrap metal. Appendix 3.6 contains an example of guidelines for dealing with scrap metal.

Stage 4 — Processing

The success of a recycling program is often directly related to the amount of processing done on the separated materials. Processing in the context of recycling almost always involves increasing the density of the recyclables. Granulating plastic, for example, increases its density by up to twenty times. This means that a given storage capacity in a building, or shipping volume in a truck, will carry twenty times as much weight of plastic after granulating. The granulated form is far more marketable.

In addition to plastics granulation, other processing includes baling, chipping, crushing, shredding, disassembly, and mixing. Each is discussed in turn. Appendix 3.5 contains a representative listing of dealers of equipment for these most common types of processing.

Baling. Industrial balers are frequently used in recycling programs. Making bales of roughly 1.5 cubic yards, this handy piece of equipment is commonly used on newspaper, cardboard, and plastic bottles, although it can also be used to bale tin and aluminum cans, other plastics, other paper products, and even light metals. Specialized balers are available for heavy metal scrap. The latter are more likely to be used by dealers in scrap metal than recycling centers. Since heavy scrap is already dense, local centers find that it is more economical to focus baling on low density materials.

Since the resulting bales weigh at least several hundred pounds, a small forklift is commonly needed. In addition, of course, the baler will need a solid cement floor and will have to be protected from the weather. Balers cost $8,000 to $30,000. Appendix 3.5D provides more detail on the various types of industrial balers.

Granulating. For PET and HDPE, plastic granulation is an option. The cost of granulators is modest, and the resulting densification is impressive. One-gallon milk jugs are just piles of stuff until granulation turns them into an easily packaged and stored commodity that is also fairly easy to market.

There are two drawbacks to granulation. A granulator is a very specialized piece of equipment. Although a baler is more expensive, it can handle a much larger variety of materials. In most cases a baler would be the first choice of processing equipment, and a granulator or other specialized machine would be the second. A second drawback, which has been alluded to, is that granulated plastic can be contaminated easily. One small piece of tin, aluminum, lead, or some nonequivalent plastic, granulated by mistake, can ruin a whole gaylord of plastic. With a granulator, the monitoring of separated materials becomes crucial, and maintaining a physical barrier between the recyclers and the machine is very important so they cannot feed the machine. For safety reasons, this is a good idea in any case.

Glass Crushing. With glass, as with most other separated materials, it is important to increase its density to reduce storage space and facilitate marketing. Although it may seem that the simple tossing of glass bottles into bins will cause substantial breakage and hence adequate densification, this in fact is not the case. Without a strenuous and dangerously high degree of effort on the part of an attendant—the danger is from shattering glass—a significant amount of breakage cannot be achieved. A much safer and considerably more effective means of reducing the volume of glass is with a glass crusher. Such devices are quite simple and can be purchased for several thousand dollars.

Glass is costly to move and presents a hazard to both humans and machinery. It is advised, therefore, that the bins or dumpsters toward which the glass-crusher output is directed also be the storage space for the glass. The glass could be loaded from this bin or dumpster directly into the buyer's truck without further handling. The loading of glass provides the strongest argument for having a forklift that can be easily converted to a bucket loader.

Chipping. The disposal of brush and tree limbs is a common problem, not only for municipalities but also in any situation where there are grounds to be taken care of. A chipper for such material is often useful and cost-effective since the resulting material can be used (or sold) as mulch or can be incorporated into a composting program. Composting generates a considerably upgraded product, which is often bagged and sold on site.

Disassembly. With the greatly increased value of metals and the consequent development of specialized buyers, the disassembly of multimaterial metal products has become much more common. The ultimate example is the development of disassembly lines by BMW of Germany for the purpose of recovering parts from used cars. In a recycling facility in this country, disassembly may involve removing capacitors, tubing, and motors from refrigerators, webbing from aluminum lawn chairs, tires from bicycles and lawn mowers, or nails from reusable lumber. This tends to be a very labor-intensive activity and a variety of common hand tools, as well as specialized snippers and cutters, will be required.

Mixing. Any recycling operation that has a composting component will greatly increase the efficacy of the composting by frequently mixing the compost pile. This is particularly important for rodent and odor control if food waste is incorporated in the mixture. The bucket loader used in glass loading can be used to mix up the compost pile (after washing off glass residue, of course). Specialized mixing equipment is also available.

Other Processing. There are many other types of specialized processing. Scrap metal, for example, is often shredded or baled with very heavy duty machinery, and newspaper can be shredded at a recycling center for sale to local farmers or kennels as animal bedding. Local recycling centers develop amazingly creative means for increasing the density or purity of separated materials in order to enhance their marketability.

Stages 5 and 6 — Storage and Transportation

Storage and transportation are considered together because proper storage (after proper processing) will encourage buyers to come to your facility and hence greatly reduce your transportation costs. Marketing contracts often require that the materials be processed in certain ways (baled, granulated, or crushed, for example). The material in its processed state also must often be accumulated to certain amounts to make it attractive to buyers. Thus, one might need a trailer truckload of bales of HDPE plastic in order to induce an acceptable price at the dock. The argument for having protected space for storage is very strong, and it is difficult to picture a recycling center that doesn't have at least one building (if for nothing else than to keep the machinery out of the weather). Covered spaces other than buildings can be used, of course, including old boxcars and trailer boxes, cement bins with canvas tops (for glass perhaps), and covered dumpsters. Recycling centers are excellent ways to recycle old buildings such as warehouses, railway depots, highway garages, barns, factories, and the like. Since the demands on the building itself are very modest, often a roof and walls are all that are needed.

TRACK 2 (MRF) RECYCLING

The technology described thus far covered the large number of situations in which separation was done at the source. This separation could be done by household members in the kitchen, by sanitation workers at curbside, by office workers at their desks, or by clerks in a department store. The key is that it was done close to the source and had to be done by hand. An alternative to this source-specific separation (SSS), and one now found at more than 100 sites around the country, is the material recovery facility, or MRF. There are many variations on the MRF, but the most common characteristic is that recyclables are ultimately sorted primarily by machine. They come to a central facility in a commingled state and are specifically separated in an assembly-line fashion by any and all of a series of magnets, screens, air blowers, and/or hand labor. The separated materials are baled, granulated, crushed, and so on as described under Track 1.

A claimed advantage of the MRF is that it will increase participation at the source because the people who do the separating—household or dorm residents, office workers, clerks, hospital staff—only have to put all recyclables together (commingled) in one receptacle, and MRF does the final sorting. No one seems to have offered evidence that this seemingly easier separation raises participation rates, however. A common variation is that paper and "all other recyclables" are separated at the source and then each is further separated at the MRF. A second advantage of a MRF-based system is that fewer containers are needed, both in the source buildings and in the trucks doing pickups, whether at curbside or otherwise.

There are several disadvantages to a recycling track involving a MRF. An often-significant capital expenditure is necessary. This would involve a building and any of a number of various combinations of assembly lines, magnets, screens, and so on. MRFs are therefore found where relatively large populations can be served effectively. A second disadvantage is the generation of residues (mainly broken glass) of up to 20 percent of the material brought in, and these must normally be disposed of as trash. A third disadvantage is found in the safety area. Hand sorters on an assembly line are exposed to somewhat more of a safety hazard than that found in the batch-processing from source-specific separation. Appendix 3.1 contains a listing of operating MRFs, and Appendix 3.2 lists dealers selling MRFs and related equipment.

TRACK 3 (MWP) RECYCLING

A recent development in the solid waste/recycling field is the mixed waste processor. Although some observers view these as a variation on a MRF, it is based on a fundamentally different view of waste disposal. Under source-specific separation or source-commingled separation (associated with a MRF), those at the source take some responsibility for their role in waste production. They participate in recycling through some type of separation. The mixed waste processor simply takes unsorted trash and searches it for recyclables. By its very nature it must be more complicated than a MRF because it has a much more difficult task. The use of larger numbers and sizes of screens, trommels, and baffles is common to try to filter out potential recyclables.

In addition to the philosophical problem related to no involvement by people at the source, there are other significant problems with mixed waste processing. At best such facilities are promising to extract only 25 percent of the waste stream (Apotheker, 1991, p. 32). And a big problem is the purity of these recyclables. Many buyers reject them because the contamination from having been part of the trash stream is too high. Safety is also a significant concern. Hand sorting through a stream of mixed waste can present major hazardous waste dangers for employees.

Although mixed waste processors may provide a useful service where it is not possible to do source separation or perhaps in mining old landfills, it is difficult to see a role for them when thinking of recycling as something that raises peoples' environmental awareness. Appendix 3.4 contains a list of operating or planned mixed waste processors.

SUMMARY

In Chapter 3 recycling was presented in detail as a process often containing a number of important steps, or stages. Examples were separation, accumulation, processing, and storage. Good recycling programs must be planned carefully to include these functions and more. It was also shown that materials handling and several types of monitoring were crucial parts of successful recycling. Although the focus was on separation at the source, note was also made of newer, more mechanized separation techniques. The materials recovery facility and the mixed waste processor were examples of these technologies. The problem of excess residues was noted as a drawback with both and of particular concern with the latter.

The last planning skill needed to set up a successful recycling program is knowing how to properly measure the costs and benefits of recycling. The next chapter, probably the most important in the book, shows the reader the proper accounting techniques for recycling.

4

How to Measure the Gains from Recycling

This chapter provides the last and perhaps most important activity in the planning process: how to use simple financial concepts to evaluate the items in the waste stream to see if they are worth recycling. Although the focus is on monetary costs and benefits, it should be noted that there are nonmonetary costs and benefits from recycling as well. An example of a nonmonetary cost is much of the recyclable separation done in households and offices; an example of a nonmonetary benefit is the cleaner environment that comes with reduced solid waste disposal. However, the focus here is on dollar costs and benefits because the primary aim of this book is to show how recycling can be evaluated within the normal solid waste management budgeting process.

To correctly project the costs and benefits from recycling, it is necessary to know a waste stream in detail and what equipment and labor will be needed to separate and process it. Such information has been derived from the guidance given in Chapters 2 and 3. Combined with actual labor and capital costs and market prices of the various recycled materials, this yields the basic financial data to determine the costs and benefits of recycling. What is left is knowing how to use the data.

MONETARY BENEFITS FROM RECYCLING

There are two significant dollar benefits from recycling. Although the sale of recovered materials (or the difficulties thereof) is much discussed, it is often a minor consideration. Frequently, a much more substantial gain from recycling is the so-called cost avoided gain. Every time a ton of material is removed from the waste stream (i.e., separated out for recycling), the fee for disposing of that ton as trash is saved. This savings is called *costs avoided* and since trash disposal costs are rising rapidly, the potential for such saving is rising accordingly. In the recycling of many materials, this is the benefit that makes the program cost-effective. The $100 or more per ton for trash disposal is saved, even if the separated materials are given away. The evaluation of a municipal recycling program in Chapter 7 shows that in such a program, cost avoided savings are about 75 percent of the total gain from recycling.

Savings from Costs Avoided

Each ton of recyclables removed from the waste stream of a town, institution, or firm reduces solid waste disposal by the amount it takes to process, transport, and dispose of that ton as trash. The gains from costs avoided often have to be carefully adapted to each situation since there are many different trash disposal processes. It is helpful to discuss these gains with reference to the four general types of costs associated with getting rid of trash (as opposed to processing recyclables, discussed in Chapter 3); these categories of costs are for collection, processing, transportation, and disposal. Of course in some trash disposal situations there is only one fee to the generator of the waste; a trash contractor simply comes and takes it away. The other costs are included in the fee charged by the hauler. At the other extreme are situations in which all four types of costs have to be covered separately and explicitly. To measure what we are avoiding, we must understand what these costs are.

Collection. A major factor regarding collection costs is how the trash moves in the system, from its production points in numerous spots within households, firms, and institutions to central locations where in a loaded form it is ready to be taken to a final disposal site. (The term *final disposal site* can be a little misleading. For some of the trash, it is wherever air currents take particulates from an incinerator, wherever the incinerator ash is landfilled, or wherever the leachate from a landfill ends up.) Many methods exist for this process, ranging simply from loading a dumpster at the point of trash production and then hauling it to the disposal site, to a complicated system by which trash is picked up or swept up over a large indoor or outdoor area and then accumulated at several increasingly larger sites (often compacted in the process) before being loaded for haulage to the final disposal point.

The cost of collecting trash should fall with the implementation of a recycling program, regardless of which collection process is used. In all cases, there will be fewer tons of trash to collect and dispose of. Specific examples of cost savings could be in janitorial services, dumpster rental, and reduced transportation costs (in a multistage collection process from curbside to transfer station, landfill, or incinerator, for example). Whatever the case, these are real monetary gains from recycling and must be explicitly included.

It is important to note that we are talking about reduced trash collection costs; when we discuss the costs of recycling, we will consider any additional collection costs due to the recycling.

Processing. Although it may seem a bit odd to talk about processing trash, in many disposal systems processing is an important consideration. Compared to other materials requiring heavy-duty trucking (gravel, sand, concrete, stone, etc.), trash does not normally present a weight problem; therefore, it makes sense to compact it for hauling. Volume, not weight, is usually the limiting factor for transportation, so trash should be made as dense as possible. With a reduction in the amount of trash because of the materials pulled out for recycling, cost reductions are possible in the processing of trash. These savings could come from reductions in the number or size of the compactors, the number of specialized trucks, or the amount of labor associated with trash compaction. In any case such savings should be tallied up on a per-ton basis and added as a benefit to recycling.

Transportation. Although there may be transportation costs associated with collection, we are talking here about the cost of hauling, in final form, processed (or unprocessed) trash to its ultimate disposal site. As the number of local disposal sites diminishes, transportation costs to regional landfills or incinerators become substantial. (Remember the wandering trash barge of a few years back.) This is why we must consider transportation to the disposal site as separate from transportation as part of collection. The cost saving as recycling leads to fewer trips of this sort should be credited to the recycling program. Transportation costs, if any, for the separated materials will of course have to be added in the section on costs associated with recycling.

Disposal Fees. Fees charged at landfills or incinerators—tipping fees—represent in many cases the largest cost of trash disposal. In 1991, for example, such fees ranged from $40 to $110 a ton for residential trash at the five modern disposal sites (trash-to-energy plants or lined landfills) in New Hampshire. Since the weighing must be done explicitly to figure the fees, it is easy to calculate the tipping costs avoided. Often there is more than one tipping fee, depending on the type of material being disposed of and perhaps other factors. As an example, Table 4.1 lists the schedule of fees for the Windham County, Vermont, landfill. For comparing fees based on weight, $14 per cubic yard is about $42 per ton (using the typical 3 to 1 ratio for mixed household trash).

The calculation of disposal costs avoided is more complicated if a town has its own landfill. Landfills are usually rated for a certain number of cubic yards, so recycling programs obviously will extend landfill life. If we were to assume, for example, that a recycling program were going to extend a landfill's life from four years to eight years, the cost avoided gain would be calculated as the sum of the following three gains. (See the section later in the chapter for a more complete discussion of *value today,* commonly called *present value.)*

Table 4.1
Tipping Fees for Windham, Vt., Solid Waste Management District
(Effective July 1, 1991)

Item No.	Description	Tipping Fee ($)
1	General Tipping Fee	14.00/cubic yard
2	Burning Pit	4.00/cubic yard
3	Bicycles	2.00 each
4	Less than 1 Cubic Yard	7.00 minimum
5	Batteries	3.00 each
6	Tires, Small	2.00 each
7	Tires, (9:00 X 20 and Larger)	6.00 each
8	Appliances	12.00 each
9	Commercial Metals	12.00/cubic yard
10	Lawn Mowers	6.00 each
11	Separated Demolition Material	12.00/cubic yard
12	Wooden Pallets	1.00/cubic yard
13	Leaves in Bags	5.00/cubic yard
14	Leaves, Loose	2.00/cubic yard
15	Non-Member Fees	28.00/cubic yard
16	Mixed Demolition	18.00/cubic yard
17	Sludge	24.00/cubic yard
18	Rubber	24.00/cubic yard
19	Asbestos	24.00/cubic yard
20	Capacitors/Ballasts	6.00 each
21	Used Oil (Commercial/Non-Member)	.50/gallon
22	Tires, Off-Road/Loader	25.00 each

Source: Windham, Vt., Solid Waste Management District, February 1, 1991.

1. the value today of putting off the expense of a new landfill for four more years.
2. the value today of having to start hauling to a distant site eight years from now instead of four years from now (if a new local landfill cannot be built).
3. the value today of putting off for four years the cost (often substantial) of closing the old landfill.

If the town, firm, or institution has its own incinerator or pays to take its trash to an incinerator, a number of new considerations must be dealt with:

- If it is a small, older incinerator and the town has temporary storage for trash, the analysis would be similar to that for a landfill, with the life of the incinerator and the ash landfill both extended by recycling.

- If the trash is burned in a trash-to-energy plant, a significant problem arises. Some of the materials that provide good, or at least satisfactory, fuel for the plant also can be recycled. Obvious examples are plastics and various types of paper and cardboard. These incinerators need certain minimum volumes, and successful recycling programs often reduce the volumes below the amounts needed for the incinerator to run efficiently.

  It is a major premise of this book that if trash-to-energy plants are absolutely necessary, there has to be enough trash to run the plant efficiently, even when there is extensive recycling in the region. Under this rule and given the arguments in this book that a very high percentage of trash can be recycled, there should be only a small number of such plants. (For a more extensive discussion of the conflict between recycling and trash-to-energy plants, see Chapters 5 and 9.

Revenue from Sale

The second type of monetary gain from recycling comes as the different recycled materials are sold. The crucial importance of a careful analysis of a waste stream is nowhere more apparent than when looking at the dollar value of material sales from a recycling program. The market value of separated material exhibits wide variation. Aluminum cans can bring $1,000 or more per ton, processed HDPE plastic up to $300 per ton, newspaper often zero or less, and it can cost $250 or more per ton to get rid of tires. Of course the market prices at any time will vary considerably for each item, depending on the region of the country, current supply and demand, any new technological breakthroughs, and the degree of processing of the material. It should be again emphasized that the larger the number of materials separated, the more it is likely that price swings will balance out (the "portfolio diversification effect").

Although prices will vary according to market conditions, location, volume to be sold, purity, degree of processing, and other factors, it is helpful to have an idea of the ways in which such prices are quoted. Tables 4.2 and 4.3, although from one region, show prices for many materials being recycled around the country.

Table 4.2
Prices for Recyclables in the New Hampshire Resource Recovery Association
Cooperative Marketing Program (January 1992) (Per Ton Unless Otherwise Noted)

		Tons	Single Stop	Double Stop
GLASS	Clear	20+	$22-$0	$15-$0
	Brown	11-19.9	$15-$0	$11-$0
	Green	under 11	$5-$0	$2-$0

			Loose	Baled
PAPER	CPO			
	Sulphite		$0-call	$120-$20
	Groundwood		$0-call	$20-$00
	LEDGER			
	Color		$0-call	$30
	White		$0-call	$30-$00
	Mixed		$0-call	$0

		Loose	Baled
OCC PAPER	TONS		
	20+	$0.00	$10.00*
	15-19.9	$0.00	$7.50
	less than 15	$0.00	$5.00

(*$25/Ton if 20 Tons delivered)

		Loose	Baled
NEWS	#6 News	$0.00	$0.00
	#8 News	$0.00	$5.00

(Except for #6 News, all paper is $10/Ton higher if delivered)

Table 4.2 (continued)

		Granulated	Baled
PLASTIC	HDPE		
	Natural	$0.11/lb	$.06/lb
	M/C w/Natural	$.05/lb	$.03/lb
	M/C w/o Natural	$.05/lb	$.03/lb
	Crates/Racks Etc.	$.00/lb	$.03/lb
	PET		
	Clear	n/a	$.06/lb
	Green	n/a	$.03/lb
	Mixed Color	n/a	$.04/lb
	Any PET w/custom	n/a	$.02/lb

		Program Price	Street Price
CANS	ALUMINUM	$.18/lb	$.20/lb
	STEEL	$12.45/gross ton	$12.45/gross ton
	MIXED	Varies	$0.00

		Baled	Containerized
SCRAP METAL	#1 Light Iron	$00/gross ton	$00/gross ton
	#2 Light Iron	$30/gross ton	$6/gross ton

Source: Excerpted from New Hampshire Resource Recovery Association price list, January 1992.

MONETARY COSTS OF RECYCLING

To calculate the costs of recycling, we must refer to the stages of recycling in the previous chapter. The cost per ton of the activity described in each stage has to be figured. This will be totaled to get total costs. Worksheets with examples are provided later in this chapter.

Table 4.3
**Prices for Various Metals Delivered to Kramer Scrap, Inc., Greenfield, Mass.
(September 1, 1991)**

MATERIAL	PRICE (Delivered)
Steel	
Mixed Heavy	$50/gross ton
Light Shredable Iron	$30/net ton
Light Balable Iron	$10/net ton
Appliances (no capacitors)	$30/net ton
Aluminum	
Extended	$.30/pound
Sheet & Cast	$.25/pound
"Irony" (ie., metal contamination)	$.05/pound
Wire	varies
Copper	
#1 Clean	$.85/pound
#2 Clean	$.75/pound
Motors	$.03/pound
Wire	varies
Radiators	varies
Brass	
Yellow	$.45/pound
Faucets	$.46/pound
Red	$.60/pound
Stainless Steel	varies
Zinc	varies
Lead	varies

Source: Quoted by attendant Lou Perham at Windham, Vt., Solid Waste District, February 1, 1991. This recycling center delivers its metals to Kramer Scrap, Inc.

Before going through these stages and the resulting calculations, it is important to point out that with three exceptions, the costs of recycling are similar to the costs of trash disposal. The three differences are worth considering briefly. First, the separation of recyclables must take place (and this certainly does not have to be done with trash). Separation could be done in a very decentralized manner in households, firms, or institutions where the waste materials are produced; it could be done at curbside or elsewhere where commingled recyclables are separated by hand or by machine. A conveyor belt with screens, magnets, and air jets, as well as hand labor, also can be used for separation.

A second cost of recycling, and one crucial to most successful programs, is storage. Because of the need to accumulate substantial loads to generate decent market value and the need to protect processed recyclables from the elements while awaiting sale, storage is far more important for recyclables than it is for trash.

The last difference between trash disposal and recycling on the cost side relates to transportation, and it is more a question of form than of substance. The specialized trucking needed for carrying many processed recyclables makes it more efficient for buyers to pick up materials at a recycling center or processing facility. The price is often quoted at the seller's dock, so transportation costs are included. On the other hand, when trash is hauled to a disposal site, the transportation is often an explicitly quoted or figurable price for the officials of the town, institution, or firm. The transportation of trash therefore shows up as a positive in the costs avoided part of the benefit to recycling, while the cost of transportation of recyclables shows up implicitly as a negative because the seller's price is less than it would be without the transporation included. In figuring recycling costs, we will use the stages of recycling model from Chapter 3.

For purposes of convenience, the stages of recycling categories are combined in the following cost centers:

1. diversion, separation or extraction, and delivery for processing;
2. processing;
3. accumulation, storage, and transportation (to buyer); and
4. materials handling (including the monitoring of separated materials).

Although these categories generally follow the progression of stages set out in Chapter 3, there is an exception. Accumulation and storage are considered together because the primary cost for both often involves the same covered space (usually a building, although covered trailers, old box cars, and even canvas sheds have been used); the covered space is often designed so as to integrate the two storage needs.

Diversion/Separation/Extraction and Delivery for Processing

From the perspective of those operating recycling centers, it is convenient when households, firms, or institutions bring already-separated materials to central collection facilities. In this case all the costs in this category are either zero or simply the cost of bringing separated materials from the collection point to a processing facility. This may be much more complicated and costly if such materials must be picked up and separated at curbside or at work stations, or if separation has to take place at a central facility. As with the collection of trash, there can be delivery charges internal to the process, such as moving materials from collection facilities to processing facilities. These, of course, should be included as part of the cost in this category.

Processing

The marketability of many separated materials is so crucially linked to proper processing that it is difficult to envision a comprehensive recycling program that does not have a central role for processing. Processors include industrial balers for cardboard, newspaper, magazines, and plastics; granulators for plastic (often superior to baling, although contamination is a problem); chippers or shredders for brush and yard waste; and a crusher to reduce the volume of glass. Again, processing can make the difference between selling material at the dock versus having to pay costly transport, often over many miles. An excellent example of processing by separation to increase value is found in Appendix 4.1.

Storage, Accumulation, and Transportation

Buyers often offer top dollar for a large load. Marketability is therefore enhanced by on-site storage capabilities. This is likely to be particularly important for newspaper, mixed paper, plastics, and glass. The roof or other covering can often be quite crude for plastics and glass; even for paper a very simple warehouse-type building is more than adequate. Such a simple building can also be used to protect processing equipment, materials handling equipment, a swap shop, and so on. Provision must also be made for accumulation prior to processing. A single bale of HDPE plastic represents up to 24 cubic yards of milk jugs. These have to be kept somewhere as it is usually necessary to make a whole bale at one time.

As pointed out earlier, the specialized or large-scale hauling often needed for recyclables makes it even more important that money is spent on appropriate processing and storage. With proper planning recycling programs can take advantage of the more efficient transport possibilities available to the buyers. Taking a somewhat lower price at the dock is often preferable to providing expensive transportation to markets.

Materials Handling

Economists use the expression *fixed proportions* when an exact ratio between two productive factors must be used. An industrial baler and a small forklift are a good example of this concept. The bales weigh anywhere from 400 to 800 pounds depending on material, requiring mechanical moving for storage and loading. A good recycling program likely will require a forklift for materials handling as much as it needs a baler for processing.

An important and often neglected component of materials handling is the monitoring of separated recyclables to avoid contamination. At some point in a recycling program, the lay people doing the separating (or diverting or extracting) must be excluded from the next stage, so that qualified personnel can carefully monitor the streams of recyclables. Since this may be a fairly costly process, care must be taken in choosing the appropriate point in order to minimize cost while avoiding contamination. It is often (but not always) the case that this should take place immediately prior to processing. This will reduce the possibility of contamination from delivery vehicles or decentralized accumulation facilities.

CALCULATING THE GAIN (OR LOSS) FROM RECYCLING A SPECIFIC MATERIAL

For each material in the waste stream we can calculate the gain per ton from recycling by adjusting the sale revenue as follows:

Revenue from Sale
- − Recycling Costs (diversion/separation/extraction and delivery costs + processing costs of recycling + storage, transportation, and materials handling costs)
- + Costs Avoided (collection cost as trash + processing costs as trash + transporation costs as trash + disposal costs as trash)
- = Gain (or loss) from recycling for this material

This equation may be viewed as the general basis for the procedure used to calculate the gain or loss from recycling in a real situation.

Worksheet for Calculating Gain or Loss

This worksheet applies the benefit and cost concepts introduced earlier in the chapter for each material in the waste stream. The resulting dollar value represents a comparison of recycling with whatever alternative waste disposal system we choose. If we have correctly included all relevant costs and benefits, a positive dollar value means recycling is the least costly waste disposal method and a negative value means it does not pay to recycle. (It should be noted that having it pay from a monetary perspective is a strong requirement. Even if the monetary gain is negative, recycling still may be the preferred solution if there are sufficient nonmonetary gains from doing it.) Since the cost of waste disposal is most commonly expressed in dollars per ton, we will express all the costs and benefits that way to allow for direct addition and subtraction. If waste disposal costs are in dollars per cubic yard, they can be converted to dollars per ton by multiplying by three. Three is the generally accepted conversion multiplier for residential waste, but it might have to be adjusted when dealing with a more specialized waste stream.

Prior to a detailed presentation of the recycling gain procedure, it is helpful to set it out for discussion in its simplest form. It is important to understand the basic idea because it is easy to confuse pluses and minuses when working with costs avoided. As indicated repeatedly, costs avoided are crucial in calculating the gains from recycling. They must be clearly understood. The procedure is based on the equation introduced earlier and presented here in simple terms:

$$Recycling\ Gain\ =\ SR\ -\ CR+CA$$
$$where\ SR\ =\ sale\ revenue$$
$$CR\ =\ costs\ of\ recycling$$
$$CA\ =\ costs\ avoided$$
$$(all\ expressed\ in\ dollars\ per\ ton)$$

It is the CA that causes the most difficulty in comprehension. If they are "costs," why are they added in the expression? This peculiar calculation occurs because these are anticipated costs that do not have to be paid. Recycling is removing materials that would have been disposed of as waste. Since these are real dollar costs being avoided, they must be added in as a gain to recycling; hence the plus sign on CA. A simple example will show this point and also demonstrate the importance of avoided costs in calculating the gain from recycling. Let us say that we are recycling newspaper and it costs us $40 a ton to collect, bale, and store it (i.e., CR = $40). Further, we assume that as part of residential trash it would cost us (say) $65 a ton to dispose of it (i.e., CA = $65). Sometimes recycling centers have to pay a small amount to get rid of newspaper. For our example let's say this is true and the amount we have to pay is $10 per ton (i.e., SR = $10). Even in this soft market for newspaper, it still pays to recycle as the gain per ton from recycling newspaper is positive:

$$-\$10\ -\ \$40\ +\ \$65\ =\ \$15\ (from\ the\ newspaper\ example)$$

It should be noted that it is uncommon to have to pay to get rid of baled newspaper. This example, therefore, is a worst-case scenario.

The conversion of a per-ton gain to an annual gain—which may be more appropriate given annual budgets—is quite straightforward. We simply multiply the gain per ton by the number of tons generated per year.

It will be necessary to estimate the number of tons of a particular material in the annual waste stream. Luckily there are standards available to help. A common figure for mixed residential waste is at least 0.8 tons per person per year. In addition, it is estimated that roughly 15 percent of this is newspaper. A typical individual therefore generates

$$0.15 \times 0.8 = 0.12 \text{ tons or } 240 \text{ lbs.}$$

of newspaper per year. For a city of 10,000 there would be

$$10,000 \times 0.12 = 1,200 \text{ tons}$$

of newspaper waste generated per year.

This is the maximum potentially available for recycling in the town. The amount actually available for processing and sale would be 1,200 tons, adjusted by the newspaper recycling rate. With a mandatory recycling program and with the ease of separating newspaper, this rate might be at least 80 percent. The amount available for sale would then be

$$0.8 \times 1,200 = 960 \text{ tons.}$$

For the town of 10,000 and with a $65 per-ton trash disposal cost, the annual gain from recycling newspapers will be

$$960 \text{ tons} \times \$15 \text{ per ton} = \$14,400.$$

Put another way, this town's solid waste budget will be reduced by $14,400 because of recycling, baling, and selling newspapers. This is true even though $10 per ton must be paid to get rid of them after baling.

Although this example is for municipal solid waste, the procedure would be the same for evaluating recycling in any waste disposal situation. Whether it is high grade paper in an office, cardboard at a shopping mall, or beverage containers at a recreation area, there will be sale revenue (SR), waste disposal costs avoided by recycling (CA), and recycling costs (CR). In the more specialized and contained waste disposal situations such as those mentioned, it is likely to be easier to figure the amount of solid waste disposed of and, hence, the actual recycling rate (compared to a municipality). The calculation of the gain will then be more accurate.

Present Value and Capital Cost

Two cost concepts that tend to be poorly understood, but are important in recycling/solid waste accounting, are *present value* and *capital cost*. Since some costs (and benefits) occur in the present and some will occur in the future, we have to have a way of comparing them. For example, if a recycling program puts off the closing of a landfill for a certain number of years (a cost avoided benefit), how do we include this gain in our formula? To make a comparison between a future dollar amount and a current dollar amount, we must discount the future, since we won't get the gain for some time. The current value from discounting a future cost or benefit is called *present value*. As an example, let us say we are proposing a recycling program that will extend the closing date of a landfill from four years to eight years into the future. Further, we assume that when the landfill is closed there will be a $100 per-ton charge for getting rid of waste by alternative means. The recycling program has put off a $100 per-ton expense from year 4 to year 8, a clear gain. To calculate the current value of this gain so as to add it into our formula, we first find the present value of $100 to be paid in four years. We then find the present value of $100 to be paid in eight years. We subtract the two. This is the gain per ton from putting off the landfill closing from year 4 to year 8. Or, more precisely, it is the gain from putting off the alternative and more costly waste disposal option. The actual calculation is as follows.

The value today of (say) $100 to be spent in four years discounted at 10 percent is:

$$\frac{100}{(1.10)^4} = \$68.31$$

$100 to be spent in eight years instead has a present value of:

$$\frac{100}{(1.10)^8} = \$46.66$$

Therefore a current cost saving of $21.65 per ton ($68.31 − $46.66) is achieved by putting off the costly alternative from year 4 to year 8. There are likely to be other gains from putting off the closing. An obvious one involves the often-significant closing cost itself.

Capital costs are generally those for plant and equipment. In the case of a recycling program, *plant* would normally be one or more buildings holding machinery, accumulation bins, storage areas, perhaps a flea market, and also providing work space. *Equipment* would include balers, granulators, a forklift, specialized trucks and igloos, and dumpsters for material drop-off.

Since plant and equipment provide service for several (or even many) years, normal accounting practice allows spreading the cost over multiple years. The procedure for doing this is quite straightforward, although certain assumptions have to be made. The first of these assumptions is how long a particular building or piece of equipment is going to last. It is best to be conservative, thus assumptions in the range of 4 to 6 years "of life" are common for equipment and vehicles and in the range of 10 to 20 years for buildings. A second important assumption involves what else the money could have been used for. Common practice is to identify a financial asset as the alternative. The return on this asset will then represent what we gave up by using the money for the building or equipment. To get the true cost of a capital expenditure, we have to inflate each year's share of the cost by a percentage to account for what we could have earned. This may be 4 or 7 or 10 percent or whatever we might have earned otherwise (say by buying a certificate of deposit (CD) of the same duration as the estimate of the life of the piece of equipment or building).

An example should make the calculation of capital costs more clear. Let us say we are looking at a forklift/bucket loader costing $20,000 having an expected life of at least 5 years. Further, we assume that we could earn 10 percent interest on the same $20,000 if put in a CD. What we want to know is the cost per year for the loader over its 5-year life. Four thousand dollars per year ($20,000/5) is not correct because it does not account for the earnings we gave up by not buying a CD instead. Those familiar with the world of investments should recognize this problem as one in which an annuity receivable would be appropriate. Since the services of the loader are provided each year, we must see how much income the CD would generate each year. Since the loader is assumed to be valueless at the end of 5 years, we assume the CD will be gone at that time also. An annuity table will tell us how much a 5-year annuity on $20,000 at 10 percent will pay out in each of 5 years. The resulting amount is roughly $5,100; therefore, this would be the appropriate annual capital cost for the loader/forklift. Maintenance would be viewed as an operating expense each year the maintenance was done. Any year after the fifth that the piece of equipment lasted would be free from a capital cost perspective.

Two caveats ought to be made at this point. First, at low volumes, balers, granulators, and other equipment may not be cost-justified (i.e., what economists call economies of scale cannot be achieved). In this case regional or interinstitutional sharing may be appropriate. Second, as volumes increase, the cost and/or revenue figures used in the worksheet may change (an increase in cost because of diminishing returns, for example), and this consideration should be noted as volumes increase.

APPLYING THE ANALYSIS

Background and Results

This section contains the results from applying the analysis to the town of Chesterfield, New Hampshire. The assumptions used and the sources of the

Table 4.4

Gain from Recycling Various Materials; Chesterfield, N.H., 1988 (Per Ton Basis)

Non-Hazardous Non-Automotive Solid Waste Stream	Percent by Weight	Price for Recycled Goods $/Ton	Diversion/ Separation/ Extraction & Delivery Costs[5]	Processing Costs[6] $/Ton
		(SR)	(Part of CR)	(Part of CR)
Mixed Paper	17	$(0-13)^2$	0	-27
Food Waste	15	Not commonly recycled but can be part of
Brush, Wood, Yard Waste	15	100^3	0	-32^3
Bottles & Jars	11	$(0-15)^2$	0	0
Corrugated Paper	10	20^2	0	-22
Newspaper	8	$(0-15)^2$	0	-34
Bulky Scrap Metal, "White" Metal[1]	6	-40^3	0	-36
Demolition Waste, Other Bulky (Furniture)	6	Cannot currently be recycled[4]
Plastic Bottles (HDPE)	2	216^2	0	-22
Plastic Bottles (PET)	2	$(40-200)^2$	0	-22
Other Plastic	2	Cannot currently be recycled
Tires	2	Cannot currently be recycled
Aluminum Cans	1	1000^3	0	-6
Tin Cans	1	0^3	0	-6
Miscellaneous	2			

Source: Thomas Duston, "An Application of Cost-Benefit Analysis," 1989, p. 3.

1. Scrap iron and white goods are listed together because they are disposed of together. Scrap iron alone, if separated, can be sold on site (see Appendix 4.1); white goods (metal appliances), however, are costly to dispose of, although the motors and the tubing may have value. Various non-ferrous metals (particularly copper) may be quite common in areas where considerable building renovation is taking place.
2. Baled and stored in appropriate amounts; New Hampshire Resource Recovery Association Price List for 1988.
3. Estimate.

Storage/Transportation & Materials Handling Costs When Recycled[7] $/Ton	Collection Costs as Trash $/Ton	Processing Cost for Trash[8] $/Ton	Transportation of Trash[9] $/Ton	Disposal Fee for Trash[10] $/Ton	Gain from Recycling $/Ton
(Part of CR)	(Part of CA)	(Part of CA)	(Part of CA)	(Part of CA)	
-34	0	9	10	50	8-21

a municipal composting plan.

0	0	9	10	50	137[3]
-15	0	9	10	50	54-69
-5	0	9	10	50	62
-6	0	9	10	50	29-44
0	0	9	10	50	-7[3]
-5	0	9	10	50	270
-5	0	9	10	50	82-242
0	0	9	10	50	1063[3]
0	0	9	10	50	63[3]

4. Some demolition waste and furniture can be reused.
5. Materials are brought, already separated, to recycling center by households. Trash is also brought by households.
6. See discussion that follows for derivation of processing costs.
7. See discussion that follows for derivation of storage costs.
8. Compaction to increase density for hauling.
9. Assume 50-mile round-trip at $2 per mile, 10-ton load.
10. Tipping fees at a landfill.

market prices are given. Techniques for determining storage costs, processing costs, and so forth are explained in the definitions for Table 4.4. The dollar values appearing in Table 4.4 are calculated as explained earlier in the chapter. The total gain for each material is found by multiplying the per-ton gain by the number of tons in any particular waste stream. Among other things, this approach is helpful in determining which items should be recycled in each specific situation.

The markets for recyclables are quite volatile. The cost of trash disposal is generally rising, and the supply of recycling equipment and technologies is expanding and changing. Therefore, Table 4.4 is for illustrative purposes only, and the values should not be used as estimates of current conditions. A good example of rapid change is within the entry called *bulky metal scrap and white goods*. When this table was generated in 1988, these materials were often losers as far as recycling was concerned. By 1992 many of the materials in these two categories were being recycled.

Definitions of Materials in Table 4.4

Mixed Paper. This is a catchall category that can include all paper, but usually includes only paper that is not otherwise worth separating. Therefore, newspaper, corrugated cardboard, white paper, computer paper, and sometimes magazines are separated out because they have a higher value processed alone than as part of mixed paper. Generally, other attached or associated materials, such as wax paper, plastic wrapping, and so on cannot be included with mixed paper and must be removed. Mixed paper is very likely to have to be baled and accumulated to significant amounts to be marketable.

Food Waste. Properly managed, food wastes can be incorporated in municipal composting programs. They can also be composted by households.

Brush, Wood, Yard Waste. Either directly or after chipping, these items can be composted outdoors with very little management. The inclusion of food wastes requires a somewhat higher level of management. Used lumber is generally not acceptable for composting because it may contain paint, nails, preservatives, and so forth. Composted materials are often bagged and sold on-site.

Glass Bottles and Jars. Generally these have to be separated into clear, brown, and green and accumulated for sale in multiton loads. Crushing is recommended as it increases marketability. Because of the difficulty in moving glass around, it is recommended that it be stored in the same container (usually a large bin) where it is accumulated initially.

Corrugated. Cardboard boxes, when baled and accumulated, can generally be sold at the dock.

Newspaper. Newspaper is usually baled for sale and in truckload lots can often be sold at the dock. The price does vary considerably, so it is sometimes necesssary to transport it someplace for sale. As trash it often costs $50 per ton or more to get rid of it. Therefore, transporting it baled and giving it away often provides significant savings. In certain agricultural areas newspaper is being shredded for dairy animal bedding and then spread on the fields to be plowed.

Bulky Scrap, White Metal. See footnote 1 from Table 4.4.

Demolition Waste, Other Bulk (furniture, for example). See Chapter 2.

HDPE Plastic. Plastic milk jugs and other heavy plastic bottles are readily marketable if granulated, shredded, or baled.

PET Plastic. Plastic soda bottles are readily marketable if granulated, shredded, or baled.

Other Plastic. This category includes packaging materials, as well as non-HDPE and non-PET containers. Several states are considering laws to tax packaging, as it is generally difficult to recycle.

Tires. Tires are a serious problem as they cannot be incinerated and most landfills will not take them. Tire-burning incinerators and other disposal or reuse methods are being developed.

Aluminum Cans. Aluminum cans are perhaps the easiest item to recycle and certainly one that pays at even low volumes. Crushing increases value per volume but is not necessary.

Tin Cans. Tin cans are far less marketable than aluminum but in sufficient amounts can be sold or given away.

Miscellaneous. This is primarily multimaterial waste, that is, very difficult or impossible to take apart.

Calculations and Assumptions Used in Table 4.4

Processing Costs. Processing in this case study refers primarily to the baling of newspaper, corrugated paper, and plastic milk jugs, and the chipping of wood and brush. The baling and chipping processes also require labor. Labor is costed out at $6 per hour, and the life of the $10,000 baler is assumed to be five years. The annual baler cost for each item is assumed to be that item's proportional share in the waste stream among those items requiring a baler. If we assume the $10,000 cost of the baler was put in a five-year annuity yielding 10 percent interest, the cost of the baler would be $2,350 per year. This would be the annual payment from the assumed annuity.

We will use mixed paper as an example and assume a 60 percent recycling rate for all items to be baled. In this example, 44 percent of the material to be baled is mixed paper and 17 percent of the total waste is mixed paper.

1. The baler cost is $2,350 per year and 44 percent, or $1,034, must be allocated to mixed paper.
2. At a 60 percent recycling rate, this would give us a total of 0.60 × 0.17 × 2,481 (total annual tonnage in Chesterfield) = 337 tons per year of mixed paper recycled . . . $1,034/337 tons ≅ $3/ton baler cost for mixed paper.
3. Assuming it takes about 4 hours of labor to make a ton (4 bales) of mixed paper

bales, the labor cost per ton is $24. The total processing cost per ton for mixed paper is therefore, $27 ($3+$24).

4. Processing costs for other items are figured accordingly. Although a glass crusher and/or a can smasher could be used and either would probably be cost-justified, neither is included in this case study. No processing is done on glass; aluminum and tin cans are simply accumulated in large corrugated boxes.

Storage, Transportation (and Materials Handling) Costs. There is little doubt that a proper recycling plan requires covered space, both to protect equipment and to store processed materials against the elements. Also, equipment is needed and labor used to move processed materials to storage and from storage to the buyers' trucks. In this case a 1,200-square-foot building was built for $40,000, and a $15,000 skid steer loader was purchased. The life of the building was conservatively assumed to be ten years, and the life of the loader was five years. Labor is again costed out at $6 per hour. The building and loader costs were allocated according to the storage needs of each item. The items requiring storage to significant amounts were mixed paper and newspaper, glass, and tin. It was assumed that baled plastic and loose tin could be stored outdoors. This raised mixed paper to 55 percent of the material needing storage.

Taking mixed paper again as an example:

1. The building cost $40,000 or $6,343 per year, 55 percent of which ($3,489) should be allocated to mixed paper.
2. The loader cost $15,000 or $3,825 per year. Fifty-five percent of this ($2,103) should be allocated to mixed paper. At a 60 percent recycling rate, this is again 337 tons per year of mixed paper recycled, ($3,489+$3,825)/337 ≅ $22/ton for materials handling and storage capital costs for mixed paper.
3. Assuming about two hours per ton for labor, labor cost per ton is $12.
4. Storage and materials handling costs are therefore $34 per ton for mixed paper ($22+$12).

Transportation costs of recyclables are zero because the prices quoted are at the seller's dock. Labor associated with loading is included under materials handling. Equipment needed for contamination monitoring (i.e., sorting tables that are secure on one side) are included in the cost of the building.

SUMMARY

This chapter introduced the basic cost-benefit analysis for recycling. It was noted that costs avoided was usually the most significant gain from recycling. Each stage of recycling was carefully explained in terms of potential costs. An illustration of an actual application of the cost-benefit techniques was presented. The reader was guided through the assumptions and methods used in this case study.

Before learning how to set up and a run a plan, the reader must be prepared for the questions likely to come up when the idea of recycling is presented to the various individuals and groups whose support is needed. These common questions and appropriate responses are the subject of Chapter 5.

PART II

Planning and Implementation

5

Ten Questions People Will Ask

Public discussion about recycling always seems to be quite spirited, with the same general concerns raised over and over. This is true of skeptical business managers, residents concerned about their taxes, and environmentalists who really want to be committed to recycling. These concerns are typical:

1. We have so much trouble getting rid of newspapers, won't adding other wastes just compound our troubles?
2. But if we all recycle, won't the resulting increase in the supply of recyclables depress the markets and cause prices to fall?
3. How do we get rid of the stuff if we don't generate enough volume for buyers to come and get it?
4. How do we get people to recycle? Should it be mandatory or voluntary?
5. Solid waste disposal and recycling are often taken up in the context of regional planning. Is regional planning also appropriate for recycling?
6. Once we get our recycling program set up, how do we find buyers for the stuff we have separated and processed?
7. How about trash disposal? Shouldn't we get that straightened out before we worry about recycling?
8. But what do we do with the difficult items like tires, car batteries, waste oil, construction and demolition waste, old refrigerators, and so forth? They can't be recycled, can they?
9. How about the problem caused by the constant turnover of volunteers and the continuing need to train new ones?
10. We can't seem to get private firms willing to take the recycling contract even if we give them all the sale revenue. What do we do now?

THE ANSWERS

Question 1: We have so much trouble getting rid of newspapers, won't adding other wastes just compound our troubles?

First, it is probably true that the day of the Boy Scout paper drive is over. In those days old newspapers were bringing up to $100 a ton. Even with the increased use of recycled newspapers in everything from Christmas wrapping paper to dairy animal bedding, the price will probably not reach its former heights in the near future. Some of this is related to the increased supply of old newspapers due to recycling, but more about this later.

Second, and a point we can't make too often, is that the money is not the most important consideration. What is important are the costs avoided by not having to dispose of this stuff as trash. Newspaper makes up at least 10 percent of the waste stream. If all of it is recycled and simply given away, waste disposal is reduced by 10 percent. Even in the worst-case scenario, when newspapers pile up or there is a charge for getting rid of them, the town, business, or institution is likely to be better off than paying up to $100 a ton to dispose of them in the trash. The current interest in recycling should lead to a predictable supply of recycled newspaper. This fact, together with the increased concern about large-scale deforestation, should lead to new and expanded uses of recycled newspaper.

Third, difficulties with newspaper should not be used to predict how the recycling program will go. Many other materials being recycled command considerably higher prices in the market than does newspaper. Obvious examples are the nonferrous metals (particularly aluminum and copper), but include HDPE and PET plastics, compost from yard waste, high quality papers such as office paper, cardboard, and computer paper, and perhaps even glass.

In other words, don't allow pessimism with regard to the benefits of newspaper recycling to suppress enthusiasm for a modern and comprehensive recycling program.

Question 2: But if we all recycle, won't the resulting increase in the supply of recyclables depress the markets and cause prices to fall?

This question is often asked by skeptical businesspeople and indicates a very selective use of economic thinking. It is true that if all else stays the same the price of recyclables will fall as the supply increases. In the real world, however, "all else" rarely stays the same. The falling price of recyclables will induce producers to substitute recyclables for virgin materials in their production processes. Examples of these new uses are spread throughout this book and are found practically every day in newspapers, magazines, and on TV. New uses will generate an increase in demand and hence an increase in the price. This will induce more recycling, and the process goes on. Just as with any other production factor, the prices of recyclable materials will go up and down, often independent of each other. As virgin materials become more costly to extract or grow, the long-run price trends for recycled material are likely to be upward.

Question 3: How do we get rid of the stuff if we don't generate enough volume for buyers to come and get it?

This is a legitimate concern but may be less of a problem than people realize. The two most important considerations with regard to buyers are volume and processing. Although they may not rush to a site for processed materials, they certainly won't come if the materials are unprocessed (among common exceptions are nonferrous metals such as aluminum cans and scrap copper). The question then becomes, at what volumes does it pay to buy processing and materials handling equipment and to build storage space? The techniques presented in Chapter 4 help determine, for a particular situation, which capital expenditures are cost-justified. It is surprising the modest populations for which capital expenditures for processing and storage are justified. As trash disposal costs approach $100 per ton, and the average person is generating up to 1 ton of solid waste per year, forklifts at $15,000, balers at $10,000, and simple storage buildings at $20 a square foot can make sense in surprisingly low (on the order of a few thousand) trash-generating populations.

A second possibility involves sharing among towns, firms, and institutions. A local survey of solid waste generation at schools, businesses, medical and government facilities, as well as nearby towns, often shows sufficient volumes to justify sharing the capital expenditures. It might turn out, for example, that processing can be done on a local basis with a single regional storage/shipping facility. The latter makes considerable sense because of the high cost of hauling loose recyclables. Hauling to a central storage/shipping facility would occur only after the recyclables had been densified by processing. The value of the material would not be used up in trucking expenses. The issue of regional planning is taken up more systematically with Question 5.

Question 4: How do we get people to recycle? Should it be mandatory or voluntary?

The issue of voluntary versus mandatory probably generates more discussion in recycling planning meetings than any other single issue. Although there is some support in economic theory for having a mandatory program (see the discussion on public goods), most people would agree it is always best to let employees, residents, or students choose freely. There are successful recycling programs that are voluntary and successful ones that are mandatory. The voluntary recycling program in East Baton Rouge, Louisiana, is said to have a 75 percent participation rate (Thompson, 1991, p. 50). Careful planning, together with a well thought-out educational program, is often all that is needed to generate strong support in the community or at the office.

This may make the issue of mandatory versus voluntary not of great importance. If the program is mandatory, the question arises of how to prepare for those who won't cooperate. Although the author is a believer in using the positive approach, other approaches, in terms of fines, monitoring, and so on, can also be used. An example of a recycling ordinance for a very successful mandatory municipal program is found in Appendix 5.1.

The question of using monetary incentives to encourage people to recycle (or penalties for not recycling) is an important part of the voluntary versus mandatory debate. A great deal of recycling discussion, whether in committees, among staff people, or at public meetings, is directed at the question "Will people do it?" As mentioned, there is some support in economic theory for skepticism about people doing it voluntarily. Skepticism arises because recycling falls into a category called *public goods*. Although residents as individuals have something of value (i.e., potentially salable materials) in their trash, these materials are salable only when a large amount accumulates. However, the gains from the sale of these accumulated recyclables and from costs avoided at landfills go to everyone, regardless of whether they individually recycle or not. Therefore, there would be a tendency for individuals to want everyone else to recycle, but not for them to do so. In this way they get the group gain but don't have to go through the personal hassle of separation, cleaning, bagging, or whatever.

Of course if everyone thinks this way, the recycling program will fail. Because of this problem, referred to as the *free rider* problem, public goods tends to be provided only through group action with required participation (paid for with taxes, for example). In the case of recycling, the obvious group action is to make the recycling program mandatory. The author generally supports mandatory recycling because (1) it is the right thing to do, and (2) as a public good it will be provided at well below the amount that is cost-justified if it is voluntary. Positive monetary inducements may make up for this problem when the program is voluntary.

An obvious way to gain support for recycling is to use the techniques in this book. Show how a recycling program can reduce solid waste costs, thereby reducing the taxes or other expenses needed to pay for trash disposal. Even in the face of such evidence, however, there will still be free riders. To counteract this problem, a good public education program, showing the monetary and environmental gains, could reduce the number of nonparticipants. Numerous and creative awards have been used to encourage participation and generate positive publicity. These usually involve opening up trash bags at random and giving a prize of some kind to the "trash producer" if there are no recyclables in the bag. At another level, recycling programs in the schools will often have a positive effect on recycling in the households. Appendix 5.2 is an example of a very well-received school education program, and Appendix 5.3 is a listing of additional educational materials for recycling. In an office building, awards could be given to those departments having the highest percentages of separated paper. At a college or university, sororities, fraternities, or dormitories could be rewarded for the highest rate of participation. Publicizing the dollar savings from recycling will give added encouragement.

If the program is mandatory, the monetary inducements are likely to be in the form of fines for nonparticipation. It has been the author's experience that such fines should be used only after other types of inducements have failed. A positive approach seems to work better than a threat, and the program should be presented as something that is the right thing to do, a chance for community cooperation, and a chance to hold the line on solid waste disposal costs. It is hoped the existence of a significant fine for nonparticipation will be enough to signal that recycling is important and should be taken seriously by all members of the recycling population.

The bag-and-tag program has been used in a number of places to address the free rider problem: The only way people can dispose of trash is in special bags that are for sale around town. Making the price of the bags represent the true cost of getting rid of that volume of trash is illustrative. It gives people a strong incentive to reduce their trash generation and to increase their recycling.

There are situations in which a mandatory/voluntary choice is either not available or not as relevant. One example is a recycling program for customers in a shopping mall; there could be recycling bins and signs all over the place, but requiring shoppers to recycle is a bit difficult to envision. An example where choice is probably not relevant would be an office building paper recycling program. Management says "recycle" and the employees recycle.

It is claimed that requiring people to recycle is more of a problem in large cities. There is evidence to the contrary, in Newark, New Jersey, and Pittsburgh, Pennsylvania. Newark is recycling more than 50 percent of its waste, and Pittsburgh claims participation rates in excess of 70 percent (Thompson, 1991, p. 49). The material recovery facilities (MRFs) discussed in Chapter 3 are certainly an option for larger municipalities. Even mixed waste processing (MWP) is a possibility, although it presents many problems with worker safety and contaminated recyclables. It ought to be unnecessary to go the MWP route, since residents in many different settings have shown a willingness to recycle and mixed waste processing assumes that people will not separate recyclables.

Question 5: Solid waste disposal and recycling are often taken up in the context of regional planning. Is regional planning also appropriate for recycling?

There are several possibilities for cooperation among recyclers. The first is joint buying of processing equipment for recyclables. Perhaps less obvious, but still potentially helpful, is joint marketing. Other examples might be collaboration in accumulation, storage, and pickup, sharing hauling equipment, and specialization by material at different facilities.

The question of the appropriate scale for processing recyclables is of sufficient import to warrant further comment. It is relevant here because of a tendency among some planners to want to rush to a regional solution in the disposition of both recyclables and trash. A regional solution would by its very nature tend to generate regional facilities. As has been pointed out, one of the most significant characteristics of recyclables is the diversity of materials involved. Before rushing into a regional processing plant (for example) we must look at the recyclables in terms of the diverse characteristics of the materials and the related costs of hauling them. Since processing is a key in recycling, and often produces cooperative efforts, a number of specific examples of joint planning can be found:

- The stores in a shopping mall cooperate in the purchase of one or more balers for cardboard.

- Several very small towns buy a mobile plastic granulator that moves among them. The same could be done with a chipper for brush.

- Several dairy farmers together buy a shredder for newspaper to be used as animal bedding.

- The firms in an industrial park buy a baler for high quality computer paper from all the various computer operations.

Once recyclables have been processed, the transportation costs per ton-mile are reduced dramatically. In fact, regional centers for accumulating processed recyclables for sale seem to make all kinds of economic sense. Although there are still economic limits to carrying relatively small loads of processed recyclables, transportation to more centrally located truck or train distribution centers certainly could be considered. The possibilities for larger scale cooperation therefore seem to exist for transportation, storage, and sale of processed recyclables. Care should be taken, however, in establishing regional facilities for separation, pickup, and processing.

Regional or interinstitutional cooperation in marketing is a distinct possibility, either with regional storage facilities as in the previous example or purely at the administrative level. An excellent example of the latter is the New Hampshire Resource Recovery Association. In the early 1980s four widely separated towns in New Hampshire (Hanover, Meredith, Rye, and Wilton) had recycling programs working but were frustrated with their inability to market their materials. Joining together, they formed a marketing cooperative, the New Hampshire Resource Recovery Association. This organization has grown so that it now includes most New Hampshire towns and many other institutions. The association handles negotiations with buyers about prices and pickups of recyclables on behalf of member towns.

The NHRRA does all the marketing and billing work and extracts a fee from each sale for this service. In fact, the only thing a town has to do is call the NHRRA and be ready to help load the truck when the association says the buyer is coming. The association also provides a number of other services such as guidance in setting up recycling programs, help with specific recycling problems, and running workshops to train recycling attendants. There is a modest annual fee for membership.

Question 6: Once we get our recycling program set up, how do we find buyers for the stuff we have separated and processed?

The search for buyers or potential buyers of the various materials should be part of the planning phase of a recycling program. When separated materials become available, one should already have made serious and extensive contacts. One must realize, however, that in a changing market like that for recyclables, buyers are the most interested when there is actually something on site for them to buy. Because of this, it is generally not possible to have all, or even the majority, of the markets set up as part of the recycling plan. This is no different than many other small businesses in which a certain amount of market risk is inherent in the start-up process. Several suggestions or observations are relevant on the issue of finding buyers:

1. Regional compacts, or various arrangements with other recycling firms or institutions in the general area, can often help in developing markets. Such arrangements permit delivery of larger volumes of given materials.

2. An excellent source of information about buyers is the directories that appear in the trade journals published by the industry group for each recycled material. The tin, plastics, glass, and paper industries each have multiple journals; subscriptions to at least one in each industry are likely to be helpful in the search for buyers (and for other information about recycling). Appendix 1.3 contains a list of these trade associations.

3. A somewhat unexpected and often very important source of market demand is the buyer who comes for a major separated material and is willing to buy or take other materials for side loads. Often buyers are multimaterial distributors. Aluminum cans bring buyers to a site who may be willing to take a few bales of cardboard or newspaper or maybe some other types of separated scrap aluminum. One of the positive side effects of this is that it may reduce storage needs. The existence of such buyers means it will not be necessary to accumulate each separated material to the amount necesssary to bring a buyer just for that material.

Question 7: How about trash disposal? Shouldn't we get that straightened out before we worry about recycling?

This is a very important issue, as it goes to the heart of three different philosophies for thinking about solid waste management. The first tells us we should just bury or burn the stuff and that recycling is another crackpot idea of environmental activists. We will spend little time on this since it is so far removed from the modern view of recycling. The second philosophy, and one commonly heard, can perhaps be best captured by the catchy phrase *integrated waste management*. The key assumption here is that recycling and trash disposal through incineration or landfilling are complementary activities. That is, we build a facility that accepts and processes both recyclables and trash. That way, we save on transportation and possibly also labor and equipment as each can be used in both the recycling and the trash disposal parts of the operation. In this kind of facility, often promoted by builders and operators of incinerators, the materials usually identified as prime candidates for recycling are those that would not burn, such as aluminum cans, glass, and scrap metal. The concept of integrated waste management is discussed in more detail in Chapter 9.

A third way of looking at solid waste, and one that is the basis for this book, is that recycling and incineration/landfilling are primarily substitutes for each other and not complements. What this means in plain English is that to a great extent we are dealing with either/or, not side by side. Much of the solid waste can be recycled, incinerated, or landfilled, and we should be choosing the least costly as the primary waste disposal method. Obviously the point of this book is that if costs are properly accounted for, then recycling will be the first choice for solid waste disposal in most cases. If we put as much time, money, and energy into recycling as we have into trying to site incinerators/landfills, the need for the latter will greatly diminish. The small amount of trash left will certainly be much closer in volume to the actual number of landfill and incinerator sites that meet the appropriately stringent environmental controls for siting such facilities.

The preceding argument works just as well for office, retail, or institutional recycling. We simply replace in the analysis the landfill/incinerator with the hauler who is paid to carry trash away. Recycling is usually a cost-effective substitute for the expensive process of paying a hauler for trash removal.

Question 8: But what do we do with the difficult items like tires, car batteries, waste oil, construction and demolition waste, old refrigerators, and so forth? They can't be recycled, can they?

Although it is true that such items present unique disposal problems, they present these problems regardless of the type of solid waste disposal system in use. Most cannot be landfilled or incinerated, and even the exceptions require disposal in specialized incinerators or after considerable disassembly.

In recent years considerable progress has been made in the recycling of some problem items. Tires, for example, are being used for fuel in plants in California and Connecticut, are cut up and laced together as dynamite blankets and temporary roads through marshy areas, and are finding innovative uses in playgrounds. Waste oil can now be used as fuel in specialized furnaces. Appendix 5.4 contains a list of distributors of waste oil heaters. In the few years, it has become more common for refrigerators and other appliances to be recycled. Even after the removal of the motor and tubing (for the copper), buyers have been willing to pay for the remains of refrigerators. Construction and demolition (C&D) debris has presented a solid waste problem in recent years at all types of disposal facilities. A study done for the state of Vermont identified thirty-five facilities in the Northeast and eastern Canada that were recycling "the waste resulting from the construction, renovation and demolition of buildings, roads, bridges, docks, piers, and all other structures" (Spencer, 1991, p. 65). Clearly serious C&D recycling is underway.

Question 9: How about the problem caused by the constant turnover of volunteers and the continuing need to train new ones?

This is more likely to be a problem in municipal recycling than in office, school, storeroom, or other institutional programs. In the latter there commonly would be one or more employees given recycling coordination, separation, education, or whatever, as part of their formal duties. Volunteerism is unlikely to be an issue wherever management appreciates all the costs of waste disposal.

The use of volunteers in planning, implementation, and operation of municipal recycling programs has a long history. In fact it is probably this identification with volunteers that has held back the movement toward serious recycling. After all, if it needs volunteers, it must not be generating enough of a gain to justify spending real money. A persistent theme of this book is that the recycling option is often the least costly alternative, even when employees are hired to do most of the tasks. Volunteers are often useful in the planning phase, and they can be (carefully) used in operations. It is crucial, however, that recycling be incorporated in a town, city, or county solid waste plan with full funding for plant, equipment, and labor. This would be a sure sign that recycling is being taken as seriously as the numbers often indicate that it should.

Question 10: We can't seem to get private firms willing to take the recycling contract even if we give them all the sale revenue. What do we do now?

This is a variation of Question 1, but is worth considering in its own right. It is crucial when evaluating the recycling option to always keep in mind the total gain, that is, gains from sale and those from costs avoided—the total pie used to finance recycling. It is usually the case that the money needed to induce a private firm to take on a serious recycling contract (i.e., something more than aluminum cans) will exceed the amount that can be generated from selling the separated and processed materials. Some of the gain due to costs avoided must inevitably be shared with the private contractor. This should not be a problem since these are real savings and ought to be available to further sweeten the contract with the hauler. There probably are as many different ways of sharing the gain as there are towns, cities, or counties, but the key to success is calculating the gain so that all benefits are included. In many instances this approach will provide funds sufficient to address the problem raised by the question.

An additional point can be made here with regard to negotiating waste management contracts with private firms, whether they are for residue removal, the running of recycling programs, residue disposal, or any combination. Such contracts should always be structured so that the payment for residue hauling or disposal declines as the amount of residue declines. This will give the population doing the separating a clear sign of the costs avoided because of their activities. To encourage a private contractor to cooperate enthusiastically with the recycling program, an arrangement can be made to share sale revenue and some of the gain from costs avoided.

The concept of *put or pay* is sufficiently important as a disincentive to recycling that it deserves a special warning. Put or pay means that one agrees to pay a certain minimum dollar amount for trash disposal (say per year). Such arrangements are frequently made with the owners of incinerators and large-scale composters, since such facilities require certain minimum volumes to work efficiently. Such contracts may also be offered by landfill owners or trash contractors. Typically they charge a certain fee per ton, with the understanding that a jurisdiction has to pay for X tons per year even if it does not generate that much. Municipal officials and others negotiating with waste disposal contractors often greatly underestimate the volume of recyclables that will be removed from the waste stream. As soon as material separation reduces solid waste to the "put" minimum, the fee per ton starts to rise. This occurs because the fixed dollar minimum is being divided by a smaller and smaller volume. A serious handicap develops because the recycling population can no longer capture the costs avoided gain, and this will work against recycling. Put or pay arrangements for residues should be avoided; they are incompatible with successful recycling programs.

6

Setting Up a Recycling Plan

In a sense Chapters 2 to 5 have already shown how to set up a recycling plan. It may be useful to bring it all together, however, and that is the purpose of Chapter 6. In this chapter the methods and skills introduced in Chapters 2 to 4 are used to help the reader set up a recycling plan with the best chance of success. Foremost among the skills is the ability to calculate the costs and benefits from separation and recycling of specific materials in the waste stream. This was the subject of Chapter 4, which additionally provided several examples to guide the reader through these calculations. One point was the need for readers to break down their waste streams into their many specific items (Chapter 2). An additional significant consideration was the importance of the various stages of recycling (Chapter 3). Chapter 6 combines these techniques and skills, together with those of planning and political awareness, to discuss the setting up of a recycling plan. The chapter is divided into two sections, the first dealing with planning and the second with implementation. The reader may note that the planning section is much longer than the implementation section; this is to make the point that close attention to planning will make implementation far easier.

PLANNING

Innumerable recycling programs have started with the best of intentions, a group of dedicated volunteers, and a bunch of 55-gallon drums. Unfortunately, more programs have failed than succeeded. Many failures could have been avoided by careful planning. Good planning includes, among other things, not starting the program prematurely. Nothing stops cooperation from residents quicker than several false starts and rule changes at the beginning. A key point in this book is that recycling pays much more often than is commonly thought, and the planning phase often determines the success or failure of the program.

An important consideration in planning is whether "management" initially supports recycling. Setting up a recycling plan with the support of the mayor, the hospital administrator, the vice president for resource administration, or other people in upper management is a lot easier than starting from scratch. It is more common, however, for a volunteer committee, a staff person, or a development office, on their own or with a "neutral" assignment from above, to do a preliminary feasibility study. If the preliminary work is done properly, in many cases even initially skeptical decision makers can be convinced.

One key issue to be resolved early on is which components of the program will be run in-house (or in town) and which will be contracted to outside firms or agencies. In some cases this may be obvious. For example, a town with a curbside trash pickup arrangement would probably be best served by simply adding the equipment, labor, and administration needed for recycling. It could be integrated into the existing solid waste management program. If a business generates large amounts of cardboard or computer paper, it may be preferable to negotiate a recycling plan with the trash hauler. A hospital that wants to stop using disposable diapers could negotiate a reusable diaper contract with a diaper service (Emerson Hospital, 1992).

Misunderstanding the crucial role of costs avoided often clouds the issue of negotiating who should run the program. Firms or institutions often cannot see how recycling is such a great deal when private contractors want so much for running these programs. Townspeople continue to complain about their rising solid waste budget. They have been told that the thing to do is hand over everything, including recycling, to a solid waste management firm and pay a fixed fee. Of course private firms want money to run recycling programs. The major gain from most recycling, costs avoided, is not a gain to the waste disposal company, it is only a gain to the town, firm, institution, or whoever pays to have trash trucked away. Strictly from a net-revenue-from-sale perspective, the recycling of a majority of items is a money loser, so waste disposal companies need to be paid to run such programs.

The crucial issue is not necessarily whether the program is contracted out. What is needed is an incentive structure to maximize the gain as seen either by those who are accountable for the solid waste budget or by those who are the separators, or both. Since these are the people whose support is crucial, they must see the gain. The question of financial incentives was discussed in some detail under Question 10 in Chapter 5. If the cost-avoidance gain is seen clearly as real money by decision makers, presumably they should be willing to share it with an outside trash contractor. If it is not seen that way, it is unlikely that a private hauler will do the job for simply the gain from sale of recyclables. In this case it is likely that recycling programs will be administered and run in-house.

A certain amount of political organizing may have to be undertaken either initially or after a plan has been developed. Such organizing, although perhaps useful in developing a citizen or employee lobby on environmental issues, need not be a major stumbling block. If all the gains from recycling have been carefully calculated and laid out for all to see, the program should mainly sell itself.

Considerable information at this stage can be found by visits to other sites where separation, accumulation, or processing is being done. It is probably most useful to go to a similar setting—park staff to another park, teachers to another school, kitchen workers to another kitchen, town workers to another town, and so forth. Often such visits are most effective when done on a group basis, and so it is recommended that the whole committee or staff participate. Sometimes such visits also generate contacts with experienced individuals in the field who can later give presentations when appropriate or be called upon for informal advice. Such contacts may also set the stage for subsequent joint actions regarding processing or marketing.

Several planning meetings ought to devote time to studying what is being done with the various materials in the waste stream. Even where there is no recycling, it is likely that certain difficult materials are separated out for specialized disposal. An obvious place to start is with hazardous waste, where federal, state, and local regulations generally require a careful accounting of volumes, concentrations, storage, and disposition by hazardous waste generators. A similar look at residential trash would include an analysis of which hazardous materials, and in what volumes, are disposed of as trash (see Chapter 2 for typical household hazardous materials). Also, a careful accounting must be made of which hazardous items are separated out at the trash disposal facility and which ones at a local hazardous waste collection day, and where the latter are ultimately disposed of. Examples of residential materials that are hazardous but do have some history of separation are waste oil, household and car batteries, and tires. Other examples of difficult materials would be junk appliances, construction and demolition waste, and scrap metal. An interesting example of problem items found in a waste situation other than a residence is a shopping mall. On the one hand, in recycling programs in residences or offices, the problem is recyclables thrown away with trash. In a shopping mall where the general public is being asked to recycle, the problem is trash thrown away with recyclables. The problem items for a committee studying shopping mall recycling would be those things like food waste, wrappers, and coffee cups that have been thrown into the can and bottle recycling bins. The study of these materials should include the cost of decontaminating recyclables as well as the labor, machinery, and facilities being used.

Once we have accounted for problem items, it is necessary to break down for analysis the remainder of the solid waste stream. This would normally include only those materials that can be disposed of as general trash. We have already removed (at least accounted for) the difficult materials. From the remainder, which is perhaps 80 percent of the waste stream in a municipal situation, come the materials to be separated for processing and (it is hoped) sale. The actual percentages of each specific material can be determined by an in-depth survey of local trash or estimates often available from state or local trash planners. In situations in which a large amount of the trash is one particular material, such as waste from a storeroom, copier room, or computer center, determining material percentages in the waste stream is quite simple. Such listings of solid waste materials form the basis for the evaluation of recycling potential. The potential obviously depends partially on what is available.

An important related note: Whether a particular piece of equipment or machinery is cost-justified depends heavily on the rate of flow of the material to be handled by that piece of machinery. Since loose separated material is often costly per cubic yard to haul around, such material should be processed (usually compacted) at as local a level as possible. This does not mean that processing machinery is justified at any scale of operation. Sometimes joint planning of processing equipment purchases is necessary to generate sufficient volume.

At this stage, estimates also have to be made with regard to anticipated recycling percentages of various materials. Machinery may not be justified at 20 percent recycling, but may be very cost-effective at 50 percent recycling. Of course, recycling percentages may also be made explicit goals of the program (see Chapter 7). The material on mandatory recycling presented under Question 4 in Chapter 5 is relevant here.

It is typical for recycling programs to be started by groups of volunteers. Although often the key to an initial impetus for getting a recycling program off the ground, volunteers are not recommended as the long-term core of a comprehensive recycling effort. A serious administrative commitment to recycling must include a core of paid capital and labor. Incorporating the funding for the recycling program in the solid waste budget is important for several reasons. First, it gives a clear sign from the decision makers, whether upper management, the mayor's office, or the vice president for resource administration, that recycling is a serious part of the waste management program. Such a signal is important, given recycling's casual antiestablishment reputation from earlier years.

At the practical level, the problem with volunteers is that they come and go. Once permanent staffing is provided, a certain stability is generated that can survive various ups and downs in local recycling interest.

Although volunteers are not recommended for the core of the plan, they can certainly be incorporated in an ongoing recycling program. Among potential uses of volunteers are:

• as part of a standing committee to investigate future recycling projects (current marketing should be part of the ongoing responsibility of budgeted employees);

- for running educational programs on recycling and environmental issues for school groups, employees, community groups, labor unions, and so on; and
- for helping out in covering high volume periods and perhaps in assisting with specialized recycling programs open only for limited hours (a swap shop, for example).

The most stable sources of volunteers are clubs or organizations such as the scouts, the Lion's Club, the company softball team, a fraternity or sorority, and the League of Women Voters. Such groups should be used whenever possible.

Planning Research

Typically initial planning for recycling is done by some type of committee—town volunteers, staff people, or perhaps students at a college. One common model is to have individuals on the committee each work on specific tasks in the research and planning process. There are several ways in which this can be done. Individuals on the committee can each specialize in one or two potentially recyclable materials. This makes a certain amount of sense. The uses of and the markets for the various recyclables are likely to be quite different. The results of individual research related to specific materials can then be reported to the committee and discussed; the group makes decisions regarding that particular material. There are always trade-offs, of course. An alternative is to have individuals specialize in a particular stage of recycling, with the stages as defined in Chapter 3 (separation, processing, storage, etc.). Given our focus on material-by-material analysis, the former approach to research and planning is often the most productive.

Investigating Markets for Recyclables. Although often viewed as the most important part of recycling, our discussions of costs avoided have shown that revenue from sale is not the crucial consideration for success or failure. It is not unimportant, but it must be considered in light of its importance in the overall plan.

As much information as possible on markets for recyclables ought to be gathered beforehand. It is often surprising how many different firms exist that are prepared to buy materials, in one form or another, once the materials have been separated and processed. As an example, the state of New Hampshire's Department of Environmental Services (DES) has published a list of "Brokers, Processors and Markets" (N.H. DES, 1991) with 106 listings, mostly in northern New England alone. Included in the DES listing is the New Hampshire Resource Recovery Association, the nonprofit marketing agent for municipal recycling programs in New Hampshire.

Among other things, an investigation of firms that buy recyclables will assist planners in making the price estimates required in preparing a sound case based on the techniques introduced in Chapter 4. Even if the price estimate is zero (i.e., the material is given away), the often significant costs avoided represent a gain. Specialized information on users of recycled plastics, as an example, is found in Appendix 6.1. This listing covers the whole country. Current prices for various recycled materials in different parts of the country are published on a regional basis in such periodicals as *Recycling Times* (5615 W. Cermak Rd., Cicero, Ill. 60650).

Several additional points ought to be made regarding the markets for recyclables. First, it is very important to find out exactly in what processed form, to what degree of purity, at whose site, and for what weights or volumes the prices are being quoted. These considerations may be obvious, but they are so important that they must be continuously emphasized. Particular note ought to be made of the issue of processing, as many programs fail because someone did not properly investigate and plan for the processing needed to make the separated materials marketable.

A second consideration regarding marketing has to do with the development of new markets and buyers after the program is running. An example is found in the case of a buyer who comes for aluminum but will also pay for a few bales of cardboard. In this case the cardboard alone might not be valuable enough to bring someone to a site for a few bales. Also, new markets will develop as a steady supply of separated materials is made available from recycling programs. What this suggests is that prices based on initial estimates are likely to be understated. They do not account for such positive developments as multimaterial purchasing after the facility is up and running.

A last note about marketing is important to bear in mind. Although there is a tendency to worry about the markets getting soft for a particular material, say newspaper, a well-planned and comprehensive program will have built-in protection against such singularly adverse developments. This protection comes from diversity. The more different products are separated, the more likely it is that negative market trends for some products will be balanced out by positive trends for others. It is analogous to the protection that comes from a diversified portfolio of stocks or in a firm's producing a number of different products. It should be remembered that separated materials in many cases represent a substitute for virgin materials, and the markets and prices for these very diverse materials are influenced by many, often unrelated, factors.

Diversity may not be possible in a situation in which a solid waste stream is made up primarily of one or two materials. Examples that come to mind are white paper and computer paper in offices, cardboard in warehouses and storerooms, yard and tree waste for outdoor maintenance crews, aluminum cans for recreational areas, and food waste in restaurants. With the exception of food wastes, these are materials that, if processsed properly, can usually be (at least) given away at the point of processing. With the cans one can always do better. Although there may be marketing disadvantages to this lack of diversity, these may be more than offset by separation and accumulation advantages. If a solid waste stream is made up of only one or two materials, it is far easier to extract and store the material(s) for recycling than is the case with a stream of household solid waste.

Researching Equipment Needs. Appropriate processing is crucial for maximizing the marketability of many separated items. The use of balers, granulators, chippers, shredders, glass crushers, and so on and the availability of both materials handling equipment and proper storage must be an integral part of any facility. In the category of materials, handling would often be some type of forklift/bucket loader. With curbside recycling, trucks with specially built separation compartments are usually important. Storage would include space not only for machinery but also for materials, processed or not, that need protection from the weather. In addition, enclosed space may be needed to protect attendants, as well as for such functions as a flea market for recyclables.

A word should be said about raising money from grants. Many government agencies, foundations, and industry lobbying groups have funds available to assist in setting up recycling programs (particularly for capital expenditures). A very early task of the planning committee or staff group is to investigate all such possibilities.

Preparing a Plan

Chapter 4 provides the techniques and a corresponding worksheet for calculating the recycling potential for each material identified and researched. At this point, a tabulation of the annual weights of the various separable materials should have been made for the town, business firm, hospital, or shopping mall. Applying the estimated recycling percentages for each material and multiplying by market prices yields anticipated gross revenue. If mandatory versus voluntary is an issue, estimates must be made for both alternatives. The revenue figures of course have to be adjusted for recycling costs. Costs avoided can be calculated by simply multiplying the total weight of the anticipated recyclables in tons by the total disposal cost per ton (including processing, transportation, and labor, if appropriate).

The cornerstone of the proposal ought to be a table or chart that projects total cost of solid waste disposal in the future with and without recycling. Appendixes should be attached to the proposal or report that show all the assumptions and calculations. If the services of a commercial waste management firm are used, the responsibilities of each party should be carefully spelled out. Appendix 6.2 is a description of the responsibilities of a commercial waste management and recycling firm providing such services to a hospital.

It is often a good idea to start recycling with those items that are either easy to sell or for which there are significant gains from cost avoidance. For municipal recycling, the sale category contains aluminum cans and nonferrous scrap; in cost avoidance are glass, HDPE and PET plastic, cardboard, newspaper, and yard waste. Other plastics, food waste, and mixed paper, among other things, can be added later. The inclusion of specific items at specific stages will depend partly on local conditions. As has been mentioned repeatedly, nonmunicipal solid waste disposers will have to adapt these principles to their own situations. As an example, Appendix 6.3 provides guidance in setting up an office paper recycling program.

If the committee is proposing mandatory recycling, or if it has already been decreed, a sample ordinance or set of rules could be included. Appendix 5.1 is an example of such an ordinance. Care must be taken in costing out capital expenditures so as to spread their cost over reasonable life spans. Do not forget maintenance.

It is important that careful diagrams be included, both of interior spaces of buildings and of external vehicular traffic. Visits to other facilities and discussions with appropriate people in the field are very helpful here.

It will be very useful for all committee or staff members to read Chapter 5 to prepare for presenting a recycling plan to the decision makers or to other relevant groups.

Once the planning problems have been worked out and a recycling program approved, the next step is implementation. The following section assumes that the planning steps have already been done. It is entirely possible that planning and implementation will be more intertwined than described here. This would be more likely if recycling has already been approved. If this is the case, most of the discussion in this chapter is still appropriate, but will not be quite as sequential. The important thing is to make sure that all facts have been carefully researched before the population starts separating. The confidence of the recycling population has a significant effect on the success of the program.

As pointed out earlier, careful preparation of a plan, given that the plan is approved, should make implementation relatively simple.

IMPLEMENTING THE PLAN

Education

Perhaps the most important function of the committee or staff after the plan has been approved is to organize educational efforts aimed at the population to be covered by recycling. These could include public meetings, press coverage, mailings, and demonstrations at a recycling center. Also appropriate might be programs in schools, dormitory lobbies, parking lots, and community and union group meetings, as well as numerous posters in key locations. Included in the educational programs should be discussions of voluntary or mandatory, whichever is most appropriate; demonstrations of how to separate, clean, store, and deliver; and a presentation of the numbers used to justify the program. These presentations, especially the numbers, should be tailored to the audience. The needs of first graders, businesspeople in the Rotary Club, and the staff at a restaurant are quite different. Appendix 6.4 provides valuable advice on designing a recycling education program.

A related effort is advertising the grand opening if it is at a specific facility or Day 1 or some such if a physical place is not appropriate. This is another opportunity for education, and a good time to have high-ranking municipal officials, upper management, or senior administrators lend their support through attendance and participation.

It is important to also think about generating ongoing support through education. An obvious and effective technique for doing this is with frequent public notice on how the recycling is going. Examples are large signs at the recycling center or at collection sites, such as "We did 32,987 aluminum cans this month," perhaps with the revenue generated from sale, or "Our trash disposal costs fell $3,456 this month." Such information could also be disseminated through schools, a monthly employee newsletter, or through community TV. It is very important that this longer-term educational program be incorporated in the original planning; otherwise, it could be lost in the shuffle of setting up the program.

An important continuing education tool is a well-designed recycling pamphlet. This can be distributed before recycling officially begins, in order to get people thinking about it. After the program is underway, it can be a standard handout from strategic locations. Appendix 6.5 gives a good example of such a recycling brochure.

Signing the Contracts

An important consideration when setting up a recycling plan is determining who has the responsibility for running the program — who will do the hiring, seek bids on capital expenditures, look for grants to assist in financing, and do general administration. It seems that the individuals or groups who planned and submitted the proposal also ought to be represented in setting up. A basic premise here is that recycling should be "hard-funded," not based primarily on volunteers; therefore the ultimate responsibility for running the program should be with salaried employees. There is no reason that the running of a recycling program should be any different than any other expenditure in the area of waste management.

It is often the case that contracts must be entered into with buyers of recycled materials, trash haulers, and owners of commercial trash disposal facilities. For several reasons, care must be taken in signing long-term contracts. As mentioned earlier, once a program is up and running, the marketing outlook could improve, so it is unwise to be tied into disadvantageous contracts. As buyers come for such prime materials as aluminum cans and nonferrous metal scrap, they may take other things (since the prime materials already have justified their transportation costs). In addition, as the recycling program expands, the increasing diversity of materials will protect somewhat against the ups and downs in the prices of each material. One would not want to lose these two potential gains by having signed long-term contracts. Such contracts should have minimum prices but also allow adjustments for price changes in the larger market for recyclables. Extreme caution should be shown in signing hauling or disposal contracts based on paying for disposal of a certain minimum amount of trash. These put or pay contracts punish successful recycling. A successful program means a reduction in the trash to be disposed of, perhaps below the minimum under contract. To assist in marketing, Appendix 6.6 provides valuable guidance in dealing with buyers of the various materials.

Training Employees

An important consideration in setting up a recycling plan is training the employee(s). A good case can be made that members of the planning group be involved because they have been close to the development of the project. They have done the research and analysis relating to each material and should know how it is processed and marketed. Those who sell recycling equipment would be expected to do training relevant to their particular piece of machinery.

Although the use of volunteers as the core of a program has not been encouraged here, they can be helpful in certain functions. The planning committee probably discussed at length the role of volunteers, so this committee could set up tasks for volunteers and train them.

SUMMARY

This chapter used the materials from Chapters 2 to 4 to show the reader how to systematically plan and set up a recycling program with the best chance of success. Many issues then arise regarding both ongoing operations and feedback on initial projections. These issues include adding materials, evaluating the program, and monitoring the separation effort. Chapter 7 covers such concerns in detail.

7

Evaluating a Recycling Program

Sooner or later one has to report on whether the recycling program is delivering what was predicted. Doing a thorough evaluation is crucial to the long-term success of the program. Just as planning was the key to implementation, evaluation is the key to future solid waste planning and recycling expansion. A reader who has followed all the suggestions in this book, particularly those regarding the proper consideration of avoidance costs and the appropriate processing of recyclables, should be able to show clear savings in the solid waste budget from those materials selected for recycling. Of course there are always unexpected disasters, but the careful choice of materials to recycle at the beginning should lead to success when the first evaluation comes around. And this success should be measurable because the initial calculations were on a dollars and cents basis.

Setting goals during the planning phase provides benchmarks against which to compare both operations and results. Separation percentages and market revenues, for example, can be measured and compared with initial projections. The actual day-to-day activities can be contrasted with their descriptions in the original proposal. Careful attention to ongoing evaluation will allow for rapid identification of problem areas and a better chance for timely corrections or adjustments. City officials, solid waste disposal managers in other institutional settings, and often the recycling population itself will want to be kept informed on how this new program is doing. Carefully measured outcomes, at or above those projected, will make it that much easier to sell the next stage of recycling.

GOALS OF A RECYCLING PLAN

As discussed in Chapter 6, the goals of the program can be general or specific, although specific is better. General goals can be "having a cleaner environment," "making people aware of the environment," or "getting control of the solid waste budget." Although laudable, these goals don't allow us to focus on specific numbers. Specific numbers matter because they can be used as a measurable sign of success. Examples of goals that are in principle measurable, and hence can be explicitly compared with initial projections, would include:

- specific recycling percentages for each material
- an overall average recycling percentage
- a specific percentage reduction in the solid waste disposal budget
- a certain number of years for the program to pay off its capital expenditures
- a specific percentage reduction in the volume or weight of waste to be disposed of
- a specified reduction in the rate of growth of the solid waste disposal budget.

Sometimes the goal of the program is not explicit but must be inferred. As an example, consider a proposal that makes budget projections for solid waste expenditure both with and without recycling. The goal presumably would be achieving the projected solid waste expenditure with recycling. After all, this must have been the projection that formed the basis for the initial approval of the program.

The major theme of this book is that properly planned recycling programs can often project explicit and desirable outcomes. An explicit evaluation can show how these outcomes demonstrate the achievement of the projected goals.

Assumptions as Goals

Assumptions and goals often are the same thing. For example, if we wish to estimate the yearly revenue from recycling aluminum cans, we have to make an assumption of what percentage of aluminum cans will be separated. In a sense we also have established a goal for aluminum can separation, because if this assumed percentage of separation is not met, aluminum will not provide its projected contribution to the overall program. This is complicated by the fact that the price of aluminum might change. We could meet our revenue projections with a lower-than-anticipated recycling percentage, but a higher selling price. If the recycling percentage also was a goal, we will wish to determine why it was not met and what we can do to remedy the situation. If we had it only as an assumption, we will be more interested in why the assumption was wrong. Or perhaps since we made our revenue projection, we might not care what the recycling percentage was. It appears that there is some value in establishing several different goals — such as recycling percentage and revenue from sales. We will develop a better understanding of recycling markets and the recycling population in this way. First, it is helpful to show how overall recycling gain can be determined.

TECHNIQUES FOR EVALUATING RECYCLING

Determining the Gain

Perhaps the simplest recycling program one can imagine involves a large trailer with a stiff wire mesh cage provided by a buyer of aluminum cans. Residents bring their cans to a central location and dump them into an opening in the top of the cage. Periodically, the buyer comes with an empty trailer and takes away the full one. This does not require an attendant, has no capital expense for the town, firm, or college, and can be located on "free" land. The gains from this operation are the revenue when the buyer sends a check for the cans and the costs avoided by putting cans in the cage that do not have to be disposed of at a landfill or do not have to be hauled away by a trash contractor. The only issue is whether the gain is adequate to compensate for the private costs of separating out the cans and bringing them to the cage.

To calculate the gain from this recycling program, we have to make assumptions about the number of empty aluminum cans produced in the town, firm, or college, and the percentage that will be separated and brought to the cage. We will use a modest estimate of 0.5 tons of solid waste per person per year, and we will further assume that 1 percent of solid waste is aluminum cans, that there is a 50 percent recycling rate for aluminum cans, and that the buyer is giving us $0.35 per pound for the cans. If we use a town of 10,000 people, this will generate

10,000 residents × 1,000 lbs./resident × 1 percent × 50 percent × 0.35/lbs.
= $17,500 in revenue.

If the cost of removing solid waste is $100 per ton, the costs avoided by separating these cans is

10,000 residents × 1,000 lbs./resident × 1 percent × $100
= $2,500 in costs avoided.

The total gain is therefore $20,000 ($17,500+$2,500). In this case the simple question for the town is whether $20,000 is sufficient to compensate for the work involved in separating and delivering the cans.

Of course, even in this simple example there are questions that could be raised.

How about the gain from a cleaner environment? This is of course an important consideration and would be in addition to the $20,000. What it means is that those people who value a cleaner environment more than the cost of separation and delivery would do this recycling program even if the cans were given away.

Is it realistic to think that there would be no other costs? Probably not.

Other costs, such as a twice-a-week attendant and a modest rental of the land, would have to be subtracted from the $20,000.

Determining the Recycling Percentage

As indicated, the recycling percentage may itself be a goal. It should be one because it tells us something about the behavior of the recycling population. The concept is simple. We measure or estimate the size of the waste stream before recycling, we measure the size of the waste stream after recycling, and we measure the percentage reduction, which is the recycling percentage. Determining the recycling percentage as part of an evaluation, however, may be more complicated than it seems. For one thing, determining the volume or weight of waste before and after recycling may present significant measurement problems. In addition, if we wish to determine the recycling percentage material by material, we are presented with the problem of exploring the anatomy of the waste stream after recyclables have been removed. This can be a very dirty job. It is perhaps helpful to give a couple of simple examples.

A Computer Paper Recycling Program. As part of planning for a computer paper recycling program, we determined that an average of 1,000 pounds per week of computer paper is thrown away by our accounting firm. A trash contractor charges $50 per ton to remove this paper as trash. The $50 covers dumpster rental as well as all other charges related to trash disposal. Our annual expense for computer paper trash removal before recycling is

1,000 lbs./wk. × 1 ton/2,000 lbs. × $50/ton × 52 wks./yr. = $1,300/yr.

We institute a computer paper recycling program and establish 75 percent recycling as the goal. This may seem lofty, but may actually be conservative. Computer paper is easily separated and often is the primary waste product in relatively small office areas. We assume a local recycler will provide appropriate separation bins and will pay $5 per ton for the paper. After one year, we add up the bills and notice that the annual payment to the trash removal company has fallen from $1,300 to $400. Although we have greatly reduced the disposal cost, have we met our objective? Remember, the recycling percentage is defined as the percentage of reduction in the volume or weight to be removed. Since the payment to the trash disposal firm is based strictly on tons removed, the percentage reduction in dollars is the same as the percentage reduction in weight. Our recycling percentage is therefore

($1,300 − $400)/$1,300 = .69 (i.e., 69 percent).

In this case we did not meet our recycling goal in terms of percentage of paper recycled. We did, however, reduce our overall solid waste expenditures by more than 75 percent. To see this we also have to account for the revenue from the sale of the separated paper. If we separate for sale 69 percent of 1,000 pounds per week,

.69 × 1,000 lbs./wk. × 1 ton/2,000 lbs. × 52 wks./yr. = 17.9 tons/yr.

We are being paid $5 per ton for this separated paper, so the revenue is

$$5/\text{ton} \times 17.9 \text{ tons/yr.} = \$89.50.$$

The net expenditure on solid waste disposal is therefore 10.50 lbs. ($400 − $89.50), and the reduction in solid waste expenditure is

$$(\$1,300 - \$310.50)/\$1,300 = .76 \text{ (i.e., 76 percent).}$$

In this case the reduction in solid waste expenditure exceeded the recycling percentage because the material recycled (computer paper) generated positive revenue. The separation percentage and the revenue from sale are obviously crucial in the example.

Additional Considerations. Additional considerations may be appropriate in evaluating real recycling programs:

- There are often costs associated with separation itself. In the computer paper example these might include expenses for bins, a baler (if appropriate), and additional labor.
- Since they greatly reduce the waste to be disposed of, good recycling programs often will change the conditions for trash removal. The paper hauler might not wish to continue at $50 per ton if the volume is greatly reduced. An alternative system or contractor or both may be needed.
- Using the evaluation as a feedback mechanism, the obvious question is why 75 percent recycling was not achieved. Although not a major problem from the perspective of outcome in this example, it is something the evaluators will ask the operating staff to be concerned with. After all, a major purpose of evaluation is to provide feedback to operations.

Most recycling programs involve more than one item. Before presenting the evaluation of an actual recycling program it is helpful to apply the considerations listed to the general topic of evaluating a comprehensive recycling program.

Determining Recycling Percentage with Comprehensive Recycling

When a number of materials are extracted from the waste stream for recycling, the problem of estimating the recycling percentage is more complicated. If we want a rough guess at the average recycling percentage, we could simply note the percentage reduction in the solid waste budget. This is similar to the computer paper example. This approach, although it is obviously helpful in showing how we are doing money-wise, does not really measure recycling percentage. This is true for two reasons:

- There are often fixed costs that do not fall when the amount of waste is reduced. In other words, the program could have a 30 percent recycling rate but only a 20 percent reduction in costs. The cost reduction therefore is an underestimate of the recycling rate.

- Solid waste disposal costs are often net of recycling revenues. In this case there could be a 40 percent reduction in solid waste costs, because of revenue from sale, with only a 30 percent recycling rate. In this case the cost reduction is an overestimate of the recycling rate.

Often it is not the average recycling rate that is of interest, but the recycling rate for each material. Knowledge of this may be very helpful in identifying materials that are being under-recycled. This could be due to difficulties with separation, handling, or cleaning and will alert the operating staff so that education programs can be material-specific. In addition, lower recycling rates for specific materials may help to explain revenues that are less than projected. Perhaps some money-maker like aluminum cans is being recycled at rates lower than projected. In any case it is often necessary to estimate the recycling percentage for each material. This process was discussed briefly in the section on monitoring the separation effort in Chapter 3. Here is a brief example showing how to evaluate the separation effort material by material:

1. Using standard tables, situation-specific experience, or some other means, determine the expected percentage (usually by weight) of each material in the waste stream.

2. Separate recyclables and extract from the trash stream samples of the trash. This should be done in such a way that every portion of the trash has an equal chance of getting sampled. If trash is disposed of in bags, withdrawing a number of them at different times of day would be a possibility.

3. (Here comes the dirty part.) Weigh the total amount of trash extracted. Calculate (based on step 1) how many pounds of each recycled material would be in this sample if there were no recycling. Now separate out those items that should have been recycled and weigh them.

4. For each material, the recycling percentage is the percentage difference between the two weights in step 3. For example, if we had 100 pounds of trash and glass bottles were 10 percent of the waste stream, we would expect 10 pounds of bottles. If we had 5 pounds of bottles, the recycling rate for glass would be 50 percent:

$$(10 \text{ lbs.} - 5 \text{ lbs.})/10 \text{ lbs.} = 0.5 \text{ (i.e., 50 percent)}.$$

5. Repeat this process several times on different days and at different times of day to get a good average for each material.

The sampling process should be repeated and the averages used to obtain more accurate results for step 4.

Distributing Capital Costs in Program Evaluation

Earlier, the simple example of the aluminum can cage was used to show how the net gain from recycling could be calculated. The gain came from sales revenue and from cost avoidance. On the cost side, we could have had such simple operating costs as a few hours of labor per week and perhaps space rental. A comprehensive recycling plan is likely to have capital expenditures as well. Capital expenditures are generally those that involve plant and equipment. Examples taken from the field of recycling would include processing equipment such as balers and glass crushers, motorized vehicles such as forklifts, and various types of buildings. Plant and equipment, once in place, may provide services for many years. It seems reasonable, therefore, that the cost of such items can legitimately be spread over a number of years. This is common practice in the business world, and we will follow that same procedure here.

We wish to spread the cost of a piece of equipment or a building over a period of time, but the actual purchase usually takes place at one point in time. What method do we use to spread the cost over the life of the asset? A common method is to start by pretending that instead of the piece of equipment, we bought a financial annuity with the same life as the piece of equipment. This annuity receivable would pay us equal amounts of money at the end of each year until the end of the life assumed for the piece of equipment. The last payment would exhaust the annuity. The annual payments are what we "gave up" in buying the equipment instead, so we use it as a measure of the cost of the equipment. Those with a rudimentary understanding of economics will recognize the annual payment on the annuity as the opportunity cost of the piece of equipment. Perhaps a simple example would be helpful:

- A baler costs $9,000 and is expected to last for six years. What is the annual cost of this baler?
- Let us say that we can earn 10 percent per year on a six-year annuity. We (hypothetically) put the $9,000 in the annuity and receive six equal payments at the end of years 1 through 6. After the last payment there would be nothing left in the account. Similarly, the baler would be totally depreciated after six years.
- A $9,000, six-year annuity at 10 percent interest would give us six equal payments of roughly $2,000 (taken from an annuity table). This, then, is the annual cost of the baler.

The incorporation of the $2,000 in the annual costs of running the recycling program is straightforward. It is simply added in with labor, rent, energy costs, maintenance costs (including those on the baler), and all the other standard costs of operation.

The remainder of this chapter is devoted to an actual evaluation of a comprehensive municipal recycling plan. The techniques introduced in this chapter, as well as those from Chapter 4, are used.

SUCCESS IN LOCAL RECYCLING: A CASE STUDY IN EVALUATION

(The material in the remainder of this chapter was excerpted from Duston and Stamps, 1991.)

Background

In March 1988 the residents of Chesterfield, New Hampshire (population roughly 3,000), voted to have a mandatory recycling program. By the summer of that year the board of selectmen had appointed a recycling committee, a group of townspeople responsible for devising a plan to carry out the recycling mandate. This committee met regularly as a group and frequently with the board. By early 1989 the capital expenditure plan necessary to run a recycling program had been agreed upon jointly by the board and the committee; the plan was approved by the voters at the March 1989 town meeting. The major capital expenditure was for a building, with lesser amounts for a baler and a small forklift/bucket loader. The recycling center would be located at the former dump/landfill, which had become primarily a transfer station, a place where trash is accumulated for shipment to the regional landfill. The town also approved increasing the full-time staff at the site from one person to two to facilitate the running of the program. The board developed an appropriate town ordinance (since recycling was going to be mandatory), and on August 1, 1989, "Operation LARRY" (Local Area Resource Recovery Yard) was officially opened. The name honored Larry Taylor, the recently deceased solid waste manager who was a long-time recycling advocate. Materials to be collected for resale would be newspaper and cardboard, aluminum cans, glass bottles, HDPE (#2) and PET (#1) plastic containers, yard waste, and miscellaneous other materials. Disposal fees would be charged for appliances, tires, and car batteries. The program had been running for two years as of August 1991, and it seemed appropriate to do an evaluation of whether the program was meeting the objective(s) originally established for it.

Although explicit objectives were never formulated for this plan, one can infer the most important one from the projections used to justify recycling to the town voters: to reduce the solid waste expenditure of the town. That will be used as the basis for this evaluation. Other objectives were mentioned, such as a cleaner environment or recycling a certain percentage of the trash, but the bottom line was on everyone's minds. In a situation in which tipping

Figure 7.1
Chesterfield Solid Waste Expenditures with and without Recycling
(Selected Years, 1987–1993)

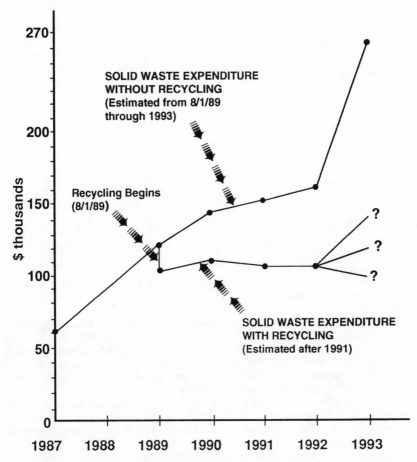

Source: Derived from Thomas Duston and Paula Stamps, "Success in Local Recycling,"
November 1991, p. 3.

fees at the regional landfill were likely to double, substantially increasing
the town's solid waste expenditures, the recycling proposal promised that
solid waste expenditures would fall in the first whole year that the recycling
program was in place. This was, to say the least, a clear-cut objective.

Summary of Evaluation Results

Solid Waste Expenditures with and without Recycling. Since recycling
reduces the amount of trash to be gotten rid of and generates revenue from

Table 7.1
Chesterfield Solid Waste Expenditures with and without Recycling (Selected Years, 1987–1993) (In Thousand Dollars)

	1987	1988	1989	1990	1991	1992	1993
Without Recycling (1)	62	92	127	148	156	163	274
With Recycling (2)			106	113	110	110*	?
With Recycling (3)			170	106	99	99*	?
Original Estimate with Recycling (4)				117			

Source: Duston and Stamps, 1991, p. 3.
*Estimated at current level.
1. Actual data from 1987 through July 1989. Estimates from August 1989 (start of recycling) through 1993. The 1993 estimate projects tipping fees at $70 a ton with the closing of the regional landfill.
2. Actual town data have been adjusted by subtracting recycling revenue and adding capital costs. For capital costs, a 10 percent cost of capital was used, a 10-year life was assumed for the building and 5-year lives for all other equipment. The assumed high capital cost and brief equipment lives tend to overestimate the actual solid waste disposal costs with recycling.
3. These figures represent the actual cash outlay by the town with the 1989 capital expenditure taken all in 1989. These are net recycling revenues.
4. This figure is the actual projection given to the town at the 1989 town meeting for solid waste costs in 1990 with the recycling program. For comparison purposes it must be compared with category 3 for 1990, as both are on a cash basis and both are net of recycling revenues.

the sale of separated materials, the town's net solid waste expenditure is subject to a two-pronged reduction. There would also be costs incurred, both capital and labor, related to recycling. Figure 7.1 compares solid waste expenditure with and without recycling for the years 1987–1993. Table 7.1 gives (1) the estimated solid waste expenditure without recycling, (2) the adjusted (for capital costs) actual and future predicted solid waste expenditures with recycling, (3) the actual (unadjusted) dollar costs of solid waste disposal for 1989–1992 (estimated for 1992), and (4) the original estimate of solid waste expenditures for 1990 with recycling. For a detailed description of these concepts and how they were derived, see this chapter's section on cost-benefit skills from the Chesterfield evaluation.

As shown in Table 7.1, there are two ways of evaluating the recycling program. One is to compare the predicted solid waste expenditure to the actual expenditure, category 4 versus category 3; the other is to compare the actual expenditure with recycling to the estimated expenditure without recycling, category 2 versus category 1.

The only full year for which expenditures with recycling were initially projected was 1990. This projected expenditure was $117,000, while the actual expenditure was $106,000. The program, therefore, saved the town $11,000 or 7 percent more than originally projected. Seven percent is actually an underestimate because the original projected cost with recycling for 1990 was built up from a 1989 estimate of trash disposal costs, which turned out to be an underestimate. The figure of $117,000 would have been somewhat higher if the increase in the cost of getting rid of unsorted solid waste had been known in early 1989.

The second comparison of interest is between estimated total expenditure without recycling and actual expenditure with recycling. For 1990 the relevant numbers are $148,000 versus $113,000, a $35,000 or 24 percent saving, and for 1991 the relevant numbers are $155,600 versus $109,718, a $45,882 or 29.4 percent saving.

Paying Off the Capital Expenditures. Other methods of evaluation could be used. For example, the number of years needed to pay off the capital costs might be of interest. With capital costs of $64,122 in 1989, Table 7.2 shows the saving generated by this capital expenditure (adjusted for additional labor expenditure). Since the recycling program had returned $98,044 by the end of 1991, the capital expense of $64,122 was paid back at some point early in 1991. Less than two years is a rather remarkable payback period.

Sale Revenue versus Cost Avoidance. In Table 7.1 the costs avoided because of recycling could be inferred by comparing disposal costs under category 1 (estimated costs without recycling) with disposal costs under category 2 (actual costs with recycling). We could also calculate costs avoided with the following two simple steps:

1. estimate the unprocessed volume (or weight) of the materials removed from the waste stream, and
2. calculate the cost of landfilling the unprocessed volume.

In category 2 of Table 7.3, costs avoided are reported for each material in the waste stream as calculated by this method. These could be added to disposal costs under category 2 in Table 7.1 to get an alternative estimate of disposal costs under category 1, disposal costs without recycling.

Table 7.3 shows that in this particular recycling program, costs avoided represent about 75 percent of the total gain.

Conclusion

Regardless of whether we are comparing actual solid waste expenditure after recycling with projected expenditure after recycling, solid waste ex-

Table 7.2
Payback Period on Initial Capital Expenditure for Recycling, Chesterfield, N.H.
(In Thousand Dollars)

	(initial capital expense in 1989 was $64,122)		
	1989	1990	1991
Expenditure			
without Recycling (1)	127	148	156
Expenditure			
with Recycling (2)	106	113	110
Difference	21	35	46
− Extra Labor Needed (3)	5	14	19
+ Capital Cost Adjustment (4)	4	13	15
Yearly Total	21	35	42
Cumulative Total	21	56	98

Source: Duston and Stamps, 1991, p. 5.
1. See category 1 under Table 7.1.
2. See category 2 under Table 7.1.
3. This is extra labor needed because of recycling and cannot be viewed as part of the gain from recycling.
4. Line 2 of Table 7.1, which is also line 2 in Table 7.2, includes the capital cost for each year. The effect of this must be removed (by adding it back in) since it is the return on capital we are trying to discover. See discussion of capital costs for 1989–1992 later in this chapter.

penditure after recycling with estimated expenditure without recycling, or calculating the payback period for the capital expenditures, the recycling program in Chesterfield, New Hampshire, has been highly successful, even when looked at from the bottom line. The lesson here is that well thought-out and well-planned recycling programs, supported by adequate expenditures for labor and capital, can bring substantial reductions in solid waste expenditures.

COST-BENEFIT SKILLS FROM THE CHESTERFIELD EVALUATION

Solid Waste Expenditures without Recycling (1987–1993)

The following calculations are for Figure 7.1 and for trash disposal costs under category 1 in Table 7.1. The solid waste costs for 1987, 1988, and

Table 7.3
Breakdown of Recycling Gains between Revenue and Cost Avoidance by Material,
Chesterfield, N.H., 1990

Material	Sale Revenue*	Cost Avoidance*	Total Gain
Glass	520	4875	5395
Newspapers	116	3525	3641
Cardboard	253	5280	5533
Aluminum Cans	3000	1340	4340
Plastic (HDPE/PET)	748	4475	5223
Mixed Paper	0	1175	1175
Deposit Containers	3918	785	4703
Disposal Fees	1470	–	1470
"Scrap Metal"	0	10,000**	10,000
TOTAL	10,025	31,455	41,480

Source: Duston and Stamps, 1991, p. 6.
*See discussion of recycling gain from each material in this chapter.
**Estimate from 1989 disposal costs.

1989 are taken (before adjustment) from town reports. It is assumed that the
solid waste disposal methods in place prior to August 1, 1989 — the start of
the recycling program — would have stayed in place through 1993.

1989 Adjustment and Estimates. (Recycling program began on August
1, 1989.)

1. The costs in 1989 associated with the recycling program itself must be subtracted
   from total solid waste costs for that year:

Total solid waste disposal cost	$170,313
— Capital expenditure for recycling	64,122
— Additional labor for recycling	5,000
Total	$101,191

2. In addition to the downward adjustment, there must be an upward adjustment
   because five months of recycling reduced disposal costs. The portion of total
   expenses reduced by recycling was primarily the cost of getting rid of the trash.
   The average monthly expenditure for trash removal for the first six months of
   1989 was $5,520. This amount would be a good monthly estimate for the rest of

the year except that on July 1, the tipping fee at the Keene Landfill went from $5.50 per cubic yard to $12 per cubic yard. The $5,520 figure should therefore be adjusted upward for the last six months of the year. A survey of solid waste cost to the town shows that about two-thirds of the trash disposal expenditure is for tipping fees. Adjust $5,520 per month upward:

$$\frac{1}{3}\,(\$5,520/\text{mo.}) \;+\; \frac{2}{3}\,(\$5,520/\text{mo.} \times \$12.00/\$5.50) \;=\; \$9,891/\text{mo.}$$

Independent confirmation of this estimate comes from page 54 of the 1990 *Town Report*, where it is noted that trash disposal costs for the first month with the higher tipping fee were $10,200. This was in July, the one month with the higher tipping fee and no recycling.

3. Therefore, an extra $4,371 ($9,891 − $5,520) must be added for each of the last six months of the year to account for the increase in the tipping fee on July 1. The total adjusted estimate of solid waste disposal cost for 1989 without recycling becomes 101,191 + 6 mos. × 4,371/mo. = $127,417.

1990 Estimate. The monthly estimate of trash disposal costs was $9,891 for the latter part of 1989. (Remember, this is for getting rid of collected trash only.) With labor costs at the transfer station before recycling estimated at $1,670 per month and capital costs estimated at $200 per month (these are in addition to the trash disposal costs) and with a 5 percent factor for population growth and general inflation, the projected solid waste expenditure without recycling for 1990 would be 12 × ($9,891/mo. + $1,670/mo. + $200/mo.) × 1.05 = $148,189.

1991 Estimate. Allowing a conservative 5 percent increase for inflation plus population growth, the 1991 projected solid waste expenditure without recycling is $148,189 (1990 estimate) × 1.05 = $155,600.

1992 Estimate. Although the current plan is to close the regional landfill in November 1992, we assume it will stay open until the end of the year. We therefore allow a conservative 5 percent increase over the 1991 figure for inflation and population growth. The 1992 estimate is $155,600 (1991 estimate) × 1.05 = $163,380.

1993 Estimate. We assume that the regional landfill will be closed as of the beginning of 1993. Alternatives to this landfill must therefore be projected as of January 1, 1993.

Regardless of what these alternatives are, a disposal fee for trash in the region (at a compost facility, transfer station, or trash-to-energy plant) will be at least $70 per ton. Using this conservative estimate, a 2 to 1 ratio of disposal costs for trash to other trash disposal expenses, and the 5 percent for population growth plus inflation, the estimated solid waste cost for 1993 under the old system would be found as follows:

- The estimated *monthly* expenditure for trash disposal for 1992 is

$$\$9,891 \text{ [for 1990]} \times 1.05 \times 1.05 = \$10,905$$

and for labor/other is

$$(\$1,670 \text{ [for 1990]} + \$200 \text{ [for 1990]}) \times 1.05 \times 1.05 = \$2,062.$$

- The current $12 per cubic yard charge at the regional landfill is about $32 per ton (using the commonly accepted ratio of 8 to 3 for dollar per ton to dollar per cubic yard. The charge for fees will therefore rise by $70/$32 or 2.2 times.
- Using the 1992 monthly estimates for trash disposal and labor/other, and recalling that a 2 to 1 ratio exists between tipping fees and other other expenses for trash disposal, the total solid waste disposal budget for 1993 will therefore be

$$\$2,062/\text{mo.} \times 1.05 \times 12 \text{ months;}$$

the other expenses for trash disposal,

$$\frac{1}{3} (\$10,905) \times 1.05 \times 12 \text{ months;}$$

and the tipping fees for trash disposal,

$$\frac{2}{3} (\$10,905/\text{mo.} \times 2.2) \times 1.05 \times 12 \text{ months.}$$

The estimate of solid waste disposal costs for 1993 is the sum of these or $273,858.

Solid Waste Expenditures with Recycling (1989–1992)

(The following calculations are for Figure 7.1 and disposal costs under category 2 in Table 7.1.)

Calculation and Allocation of Capital Costs of the Recycling Program. The major capital expenditures for the recycling program were $45,959 in 1989 for a building, $8,803 in 1989 for an industrial baler, and $15,806 paid in annual installments in 1989, 1990, and 1991 for a frontend loader/forklift. For purposes of these calculations, we assume a ten-year life for the building and five-year lives for all other capital expenditures. We further assume a 10 percent per year cost of capital (i.e., what the town could have earned by buying an annuity with the money). It was also assumed that all other capital expenditures were for the recycling program.

Taken from loan payment tables, the annual capital cost of the building is $7,288, and the annual capital cost for other capital expenditures is $3,840 for 1989, $6,060 for 1990, and $7,740 for 1991. Total capital costs are therefore $11,128 × .375 for 1989 (five-month program), $13,348 for 1990, and $15,028 for 1991.

Additional Labor Cost Due to Recycling. A second full-time employee was added at the transfer station to handle the additional labor requirements of a recycling program. At busy times part-time labor has also been used.

- For 1989 additional labor totaled $4,855 for the last five months of the year after the recycling program started.

- For 1990 additional labor was roughly $1,175 per month, or $14,100 total.
- For 1991 additional labor was estimated at $1,550 per month, or $18,600 total.

Solid Waste Expenditures with Recycling for 1989–1992.

Disposal Costs under Category 2 in 1989:
Actual town solid waste expenditure for 1989 (minus gross capital costs)
    + allocated capital costs related to recycling for five months
    − revenue from recycling
= 106,191 + 4,173 − 4,706 = $105,658

Disposal Costs under Category 2 in 1990:
Actual town solid waste expenditure for 1990
    + capital costs for 1990
    − revenue from recycling for 1990
= 108,735 + 13,348 − 9,303 = $112,780

Disposal Costs under Category 2 in 1991:
Estimated solid waste expenditure for 1991
    + capital costs for 1991
    − estimated revenue from recycling for 1991
= 104,690 (est.) + 15,028 − 10,000 (est.) = $109,718

Disposal Costs under Category 2 in 1992:
= $109,718 (1991 level assumed based on town projection)

Recycling Gain from Each Material (for Table 7.3)

The development of a large recycling program in Chesterfield has allowed the town to contract for a different trash disposal system. Under this new system, unsorted trash is disposed of at $5 per cubic yard; this is the gain from each (uncompacted) cubic yard recycled.

The Processing and Disposition of Glass (Yearly). Currently, glass is reduced in volume, all colors together, by a small glass crusher (J&R Engineering, approximately $2,500). The resulting product is used as a substitute for gravel to provide a small proportion of the cover at the town's very limited landfilling operation (the burying of demolition waste and the ash from burned brush and other clean wood). The size of the recycling building makes it impractical to store sufficient crushed glass for it to be marketable. The current price of gravel for landfilling is about $4 per cubic yard, so this is used in the calculations as the value to the town of the crushed glass used as landfill cover (since each cubic yard used saves the town the cost of a cubic yard of gravel).

Assumptions Used in Calculating Cost-Avoidance Gain from Recycling Glass

- The crushing of glass is conservatively estimated to reduce its volume by 7.5 times, compared to disposal methods currently in use for disposal of glass in unsorted trash. Ten times seems a bit high and five seems much too cautious, so instead of doing a large and costly experiment, we used 7.5 as reasonable.

- The amount of compacted glass was estimated by the employee who loads it at somewhat less than three cubic yards per week. (She moves it with a bucket holding roughly 0.3 cubic yards, and she estimates about nine full loads each week.) Again being very conservative, a figure of 2.5 cubic yards per week was used.

Total Operating Gain from Recycling Glass

1. Revenue from sale is 2.5 cu. yds./week $\times$ \$4/cu. yd. $\times$ 52 weeks = \$520.
2. Cost-avoidance gain:
   a. Volume of uncompacted glass or somewhat compacted glass is 2.5 cu. yds./week $\times$ 52 weeks/year $\times$ 7.5 (glass compaction factor) = 975 cu. yds.
   b. Disposal cost due to disposal fee is 975 cu. yds. $\times$ \$5/cu. yd. = \$4,875.
3. Total operating gain from recycling glass is \$520 + \$4,875 = \$5,395.

The Processing and Disposition of Newspapers (Yearly). Currently, newspapers are accumulated unbaled but compactly in gaylords, each holding about 1.13 cubic yards. All magazines and glossies are removed and recycled separately with mixed paper. Accumulated in this way, the newspaper is picked up at no charge and taken to be shredded for use as animal bedding on a dairy farm. As a safe and inexpensive alternative to hay or straw, this recent use should strengthen the recycled newspaper market overall. Although the containers must be kept out of the weather, storage requirements are modest as pickups are frequent.

Assumptions Used in Calculating Cost-Avoidance Gain from Recycling Newspapers

- The systematic packing of newspaper for storage and sale is assumed to compact them by three times. For a short period of time after the recycling program began, newspaper was baled and given away on site. This was an improvement cost-wise over the old system but had high labor cost due to time spent baling the newspaper. Because of this problem and the low price for baled newspaper, the current disposal method, which requires minimal labor, is a much more satisfactory option.

- Both attendants estimated about four gaylords per week of newspaper generated. We therefore estimated this number at four per week.

Total Operating Gain from Recycling Newspapers

1. Revenue from sale is \$116 (1990; currently zero).

2. Cost-avoidance gain:
   a. Volume of newspaper is 4/wk. × 52 wks. × (1.13 cu. yds./gaylord) = 235 cu. yds.
   b. Disposal cost as trash with 3 to 1 compaction factor is 235 cu. yds. × ($5/cu. yd.) × 3 = $3,525.
3. Total operating gain from recycling newspapers is $3,525 + 116 = $3,641.

The Processing and Disposition of Cardboard (Yearly). Currently, cardboard is baled and sold to the buyer who comes primarily for aluminum cans. The cardboard is mostly from boxes of various sizes, with a small proportion being brown grocery bags. Avoidance cost gain should be significant since under the current system, materials are sold uncompacted and cardboard boxes are very bulky as unsorted trash.

Assumptions Used in Calculating Cost-Avoidance Gain from Recycling Cardboard. The volume reduction through baling was conservatively estimated at 12.5 times. Consideration was taken of the small amount of compaction that would take place by accident in the dumpsters. Fifteen times seemed too high and ten times too conservative, so 12.5 was used.

Total Operating Gain from Recycling Cardboard

1. Revenue from sale is $253 for 50,680 pounds.
2. Cost-avoidance gain:
   a. Average bale weighs 900 pounds and is about 1.5 cubic yards, so 50,680 pounds is 50,680 lbs./(900 lbs./bale) × 1.5 cu. yds. = 84.5 cu. yds. compacted.
   b. With a 12.5 to 1 compaction ratio, this would be 1,056 cubic yards of loose cardboard (84.5 cu. yds. × 12.5).
   c. Disposal costs for 1,056 loose cubic yards = 1,056 cu. yds. × $5/cu. yd. = $5,280.
3. Total operating gain from recycling cardboard is $253 + $5,280 = $5,533.

The Processing and Disposition of Aluminum Cans. Currently, aluminum cans are accumulated in gaylord lots and sold on site. Because cans are perhaps the most valuable item for recycling revenue, it is sometimes forgotten that the costs avoided gain can be substantial, particularly when disposal costs are on a volume (as opposed to weight) basis.

Assumptions Used in Calculating Cost-Avoidance Gain from Recycling Aluminum Cans

- The aluminum cans are those that do not have deposits due and hence are sold for the aluminum value only.
- It is assumed that cans disposed of with unsorted trash would not be compacted.

Total Operating Gain from Recycling Aluminum Cans

1. Revenue from sale is 9,364 pounds at 30 to 40 cents per pound = $3,000.

2. Cost-avoidance gain:
   a. Average weight per gaylord = 40 pounds (conversation with Pine Tree Waste Corp., Marlboro, N.H.). If 40 pounds = 1.13 cu. yds., then 1 cu. yd. = 35 pounds.
   b. 9,364 pounds converted to cubic years is 9,364 lbs./(35/cu. yd.) = 268 cu. yd.
   c. 268 cu. yds. at $5/cu. yd. = $1,340.
3. Total operating ga$^\vdots$. from recycling aluminum cans is $3,000+$1,340 = $4,340.

The Processing and Disposition of Plastic. HDPE (#2) and PET (#1) plastic are collected and baled for sale. HDPE (high-density polyethylene) typically is milk jugs and heavy-duty detergent bottles, and PET (polyethylene tereph-thalate) is typically soda and beer bottles. The buyers of plastic require a substantial accumulation of baled plastic. The recycling program was set up to accommodate this need, so storage is available for a significant accumulation of bales made from these two types of plastic containers. Eight thousand two hundred fifty-six pounds of baled plastic were sold in 1990.

Assumptions Used in Calculating Cost-Avoidance Gain from Recycling Plastic

- It is assumed that these containers would not be compacted when disposed of as unsorted trash.
- A certain number of soda bottles (PET) would be removed for inclusion as more valuable deposit containers.
- Average weight per bale = 350 pounds.
- Twenty-four gaylords uncompacted needed for one bale (according to attendants).

Total Operating Gain from Recycling Plastic

1. Revenue from sale (1990) is $538.
2. Cost-avoidance gain:
   a. 8,256 pounds when converted to bales is [8,256 lbs./(350 lbs./bale)] = 24 bales.
   b. 24 bales at 24 gaylords per bale is 576 gaylords.
   c. Since 1 gaylord = 1.13 cubic yard, 576 gaylords is 576×(1.13 cu. yds./gaylord) = 651 cu. yds. (total plastic).
   d. 651 cubic yards would cost 651 cu. yds.×$5/cu. yd. = $3,255 to dispose of as trash.
3. Total operating gain from recycling plastic is $538 + $3,255 = $3,793.

The Processing and Disposition of Mixed Paper. Currently, selected mixed paper (magazines, glossies, catalogues, paperback books, phone books, office paper, etc.) is stacked in gaylords and given away on site to a company that makes carpet and shirt tissue.

Assumptions Used in Calculating Cost-Avoidance Gain from Mixed Paper

- The stacking of mixed paper reduces volume by half, compared to tossing loosely into dumpster.
- Weekly output estimated conservatively at two gaylords.

Total Operating Gain from Recycling Mixed Paper

1. Revenue from sale is 0.
2. Cost-avoidance gain:
   a. 2 gaylords per week at 1.13 cubic yard per gaylord is 2 gaylords $\times$ 52 $\times$ 1.13 cu. yds./gaylord = 117.5 cu. yd./year.
   b. At $5 per cubic yard for disposal and a 2 to 1 reduction with stacking, 117.5 cubic yards of mixed paper would cost 117.5 cu. yds. $\times$ 2 $\times$ $5/cu. yd. = $1,175 to dispose of as trash.
3. Total operating gain from recycling mixed paper is 0 + 1,175 = $1,175/year.

The Processing and Disposition of Deposit Containers. For various reasons deposit containers from other states find their way into the Chesterfield landfill. As the town is close to two bottle return states, these are returned for deposits.

Assumptions Used in Calculating Cost-Avoidance Gain from Deposit Containers

- It was assumed that as uncompacted and unsorted waste, the typical deposit container would occupy about 100 cubic inches or .002 cubic yards. The smallest deposit container is an aluminum can occupying about 25 cubic inches, and there would be a great deal of unfilled space when these are thrown loosely into a dumpster. Most other containers are larger than aluminum cans.
- It was assumed that no compaction of these containers would take place under the system in place for unsorted trash.

Total Operating Gain from Recycling Deposit Containers

1. Revenue from sale is $3,918.
2. Cost-avoidance gain:
   a. 78,356 containers occupy 78,356 $\times$ (.002 cu. yds./container) = 157 cu. yd.
   b. 157 cubic yards cost 157 cu. yds. $\times$ $5/cu. yd. = $785 to dispose of as trash.
3. Total operating gain from recycling deposit containers is $3,918 + $785 = $4,703.

Processing and Disposition of Metals. The metal pile, which includes appliances, old bicycles, lawn furniture, lawn mowers, old fencing, and so on, as well as valuable nonferrous scrap (except for aluminum cans), has been treated in two ways during the life of the recycling program. Initially, it was all removed for $0.015 a pound. As the prices of metals have risen, it is now all taken away at no charge. A conservative estimate of the value of this cost-avoidance gain probably would be in the neighborhood of $10,000, so this number was used for cost avoidance. This seems reasonable since a May 1989 shipment cost the town $2,590.65, and a July/August shipment cost an additional $2,042.50. The current system of giving it away on site is saving the town a great deal of money when compared with paying $0.015 per pound to get rid of it.

USING THE CASE STUDY FOR OPERATIONS FEEDBACK AND FUTURE PLANNING

Evaluation of Operations

The results reported in the case study confirmed the widespread view that Chesterfield's recycling program, Operation LARRY, has substantially reduced the town's solid waste disposal costs. In fact, the program has performed even better than the savings promised when the town approved it at the 1989 town meeting. These savings were projected to be $18,387 for 1990, and in fact turned out to be $35,409.

In terms of percentage reduction in solid waste spending, recycling produced overall savings of 17 percent for 1989 (5 months), 23.9 percent for 1990, and 29.4 percent (estimated for 1991). These numbers represent the percentage difference between categories 1 and 2 in Table 7.1 for each of the years in question.

A different way of looking at the program is to see how long it took to pay off the initial capital expenditure of $64,122. As shown in Table 7.2, the savings generated by the program (net of extra labor required by recycling) had accumulated to roughly $98,000 by the end of 1991. If the $64,122 had been put in a bank at (say) 10 percent interest, it would have accumulated to roughly $83,000 by the end of 1991. What this means is that the capital equipment had paid for itself roughly two years after it was purchased. For plant and equipment expected to last in the five- to 20-year range, this is a very satisfactory result.

Of considerable interest is the breakdown of the recycling gain, both by type of material and by revenue versus cost avoidance. As shown in Table 7.3, the overall savings is broken down in a roughly 3 to 1 ratio between cost avoidance and sale revenue. What this means is, that on average recycled material that brings $1 of revenue actually saves the town a total of $4.

Evaluation for Future Planning

The Chesterfield Recycling Program Needs More Storage. It is an indication of its success that the recycling program in Chesterfield needs more storage. As new materials are recycled, as new buyers appear, as people in town continue their cooperation, there are more things to take care of. Among the major reasons for the continuing success of Chesterfield is recycling was the willingness on the part of the town to provide an adequate building for storage. This building, which has been extremely important, is no longer adequate; a storage bottleneck has arisen. Examples of current problems due to expanding storage needs are that

- better deals could be made for certain materials if larger volumes could be accumulated (glass and baled brown bags are examples).
- additional materials could be separated and sold (numbers 3, 5, and 7 plastic containers, for example).
- a proper swap shop could be set up, and large quantities of currently discarded materials would be available for reuse or sale to dealers.

Many storage possibilities exist, with a new building needed sooner or later. Other possibilities range from old trailers to tractor-trailer boxes to old box cars. A temporary expedient would be the purchase of plastic gaylords.

An Additional Full-Time Employee Is Needed. Two areas where immediate gains could be made from adding another employee: monitoring the trash disposal system to encourage an increase in the recycling rate and managing the metal pile. Regarding the latter, at the very least an employee could separate metals into the various ferrous and nonferrous categories, record the weights where practical, and keep track of prices paid by buyers. Even appliances are now worth something in addition to the value of their motors and copper tubing. Since metals can be stored outside, volume is far less of a problem. Materials can be accumulated until it is worthwhile to have someone come and get them.

The Town Must Prepare for 1993. In 1993 the regional landfill is likely to be closed. Regardless of the ultimate destination of the trash after that time, it is going to cost two to three times as much in disposal fees than it does now. In 1989 the recycling program was just in time (save one month) to beat the tipping fee increase in the regional landfill from $5.50 to $12. Preparations must be made to respond again in a timely fashion. The board of selectmen should charge the recycling committee for this year with preparing a plan for both substantially increasing the recycling rate and adding to the number of materials recycled, to avoid a fiscal crisis in solid waste disposal costs in 1993.

The Current Recycling Building Should Be Heated. The original 1989 recycling proposal recommended that the building be heated. This is a space where town employees work many hours in very cold weather. Employee morale and productivity, not to mention simple compassion, suggest that the building ought to have some heat. It would seem that some type of waste oil or junk wood heater could be installed to take some of the chill off and to assist in getting rid of certain accumulated waste materials.

SUMMARY

Chapter 7 provided the reader with several examples for evaluating recycling programs. Although the simple aluminum can and computer paper program evaluations are appealing, many recycling programs are more complicated. The simple examples are included primarily to show the reader how to connect recycling percentages, trash generation, sales revenue, and cost avoidances. Evaluation of a far more complicated, but perhaps more realistic sort, is found in the section on the recycling program in Chesterfield, New Hampshire. Many situations have unique features, but careful analysis and a little creativity in assumptions should allow a useful and defensible evaluation in most cases.

PART III

Further Perspectives on Recycling

8

The Microeconomics of Recycling

Those readers with a background in economics will recognize ideas drawn from microeconomic theory in the first two parts of this book. Explicit references were made to public goods and economies of scale. The concepts of *negative externality, marginal benefits and costs,* and *economic efficiency* could also have been discussed at numerous places in the text. This chapter takes up these issues in detail and frames the recycling discussion in a more formal way within the context of microeconomics. Those readers with a more applied interest can easily skip this chapter. Those with an interest in microeconomics or environmental economics will find it instructive.

INTRODUCTION

The term *solid waste,* as used here, refers to those solid materials left over for disposal after consumption or production. These materials are typically either packaging materials, such as cardboard, plastic, glass, or aluminum, or residues such as food, yard, and demolition waste, newspapers, and computer paper. In the absence of stringent solid wate disposal regulations, this waste will be disposed of at the least cost to the individual, firm, or other waste generator who has done the consuming or producing. Until recently, the least costly way to get rid of such materials was by distributing them on or in the ground. This was done either intensively at dumps or landfills or dispersed through the smoke from a backyard fire or large-scale incinerator. A few things were reused, such as clothing collected by public welfare agencies, old newspapers ("broke") used in the production of certain types of new paper, and yard waste turned into compost. Most were distributed on or in the ground. From the perspective of those having the waste to get rid of, ground disposal or burning were the least costly options, and most such materials did not have any obvious positive value anyway.

As appropriate sites for ground disposal have become more difficult to find, and as the negative public health effects of air and groundwater pollution have become better understood, disposal costs have increased considerably. At the same time, extraction and production costs for some virgin materials have increased substantially. Not surprisingly, a considerable demand has developed for materials recycled from the waste stream.

The student of economics will recognize the fundamental solid waste problem here as that of the negative externality. The market economy does not force the waste producers to pay all the costs of production or consumption. Some costs can be passed on to others, and these are called *negative externalities* (i.e., external—as opposed to internal—costs). In the context of solid waste disposal, typical examples of such external costs include the unhealthy downwind distribution of materials from incinerator smoke and the groundwater contamination from a previously closed dump. It is possible to pass these costs off because the system of prices generated in a market economy understates the value of the waste disposal function of resources of the common property type. Examples of such resources include bodies of water, the ground, and the air. Obviously, since such resources are undervalued in the market, the amount disposed of in this fashion exceeds the amount that the true waste disposal costs would justify. In principle at least, a series of prices could be generated that covered the true cost of disposal for packaging and consumption residues. Such a system of prices would change consumption and production patterns toward less packaging and longer lasting/more easily reused materials. Vernon Smith discussed economic policies that could generate such a "general equilibrium pricing system" in "Dynamics of Waste Accumulation: Disposal Versus Recycling" (Smith, 1972). Although numerous and extensive pollution problems continue to exist, there is some evidence that the actual cost of solid waste disposal is moving toward the true cost (i.e., that Smith's theoretical system of prices is becoming more of a reality).

SOLID WASTE DISPOSAL IN THE 1990s

For two reasons, the system of prices that has evolved in recent decades appears to more fully cover current solid waste disposal costs. First, a great deal more is known about the public health consequences of the unrestricted disposal of waste materials. Consequently, the sites and mechanisms available for the disposal of such materials have been restricted, and disposal costs have risen toward their true social values. A second reason why prices are closer to true social costs has to do with the passage of bottle bills in various states. The temporarily increased private cost associated with deposits gives people an incentive to return the containers for recycling. In a related development, many states are considering excess packaging laws, or bans on certain types of packaging that are difficult to recycle, as well as surcharges on other items (disposable diapers, for example).

Figure 8.1
The Optimal Amount of Recycling

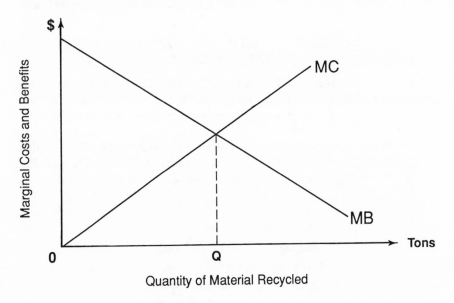

Quantity of Material Recycled

In addition, land seems to have become more scarce in an economic sense and hence the price of disposal has risen. Although this is true, it does not necessarily mean that for this reason the actual price is closer to the true price. At an earlier time the existence of considerable open land probably made the true price substantially lower than it is today. It could be argued that the increased concern for the environment has caused an increase in the price of disposal by increasing the number of unacceptable areas. Again, although this is true, it does not follow that this effect has made the actual price closer to the true price, since this increase in demand also raises the true price.

A graph will be helpful here. With the horizontal axis representing the tons of the solid waste stream recycled, and assuming we can attach dollar values to benefits, then MB in Figure 8.1 represents a declining incremental satisfaction from increased recycling. MB stands for *marginal benefit*, a more commonly used term for this phenomenon. The benefit from recycling is only half of the story; we must also look at the costs. Production processes, such as the production of recycled goods, are generally subject to increasing incremental costs (due to the law of diminishing returns). Using MC to stand for these incremental (marginal) costs, the rising value of MC is as shown on the graph. The point Q is very significant in economics as it represents what is called the *optimal amount* of recycling. At recycling amounts less than Q tons, recycling value is not being fully captured (since MB > MC); if recycling exceeds Q, it is not worth it, (since the cost of a ton recycled exceeds the benefit; $MC > MB$). At Q tons of material recycled, we would be getting the maximum value possible from using productive factors in recycling.

RECYCLING AS THE PRODUCTION OF MANY DIFFERENT PRODUCTS

Although the preceding discussion is theoretically sound, it is somewhat misleading when applied to the actual production of recycled goods. Since processing, transportation, and sale are based on the specific material being recycled and there is wide variation among them, a more useful statement on the efficacy of recycling would evaluate it in a way that could be applied individually to many different materials. In fact, Mills and Graves (1986, p. 205) have suggested that any waste material should be reused if:

$Pm + D + L > S + C$, where:

Pm = price of new material/ton
D = disamenity cost of disposal/ton
L = landfill costs/ton
S = separation costs/ton from waste and
C = processing costs/ton of separated material.

Pm, D, and L refer to the purchase of the material new, and the related disposal cost when it becomes solid waste. S and C are the costs of recycling. The extent to which the left side of the above equation exceeds the right side may be thought of as the maximum price for the recycled material.

Although the Mills-Graves condition is helpful as a starting point, it needs to be modified in several ways. Using as an example a municipal recycling program, the following are important modifications:

1. Transportation costs are often a very significant cost of waste disposal. This is particularly true with the trend toward regional landfill or burning facilities. This would not matter under the assumption of equal transportation costs for waste disposal or recycling, but realistically there are no grounds for such an assumption. Although the regional waste disposal site is in one place, there are likely to be multiple disposal sites for the recycled materials, and these are unlikely to be at the regional waste site. Transportation costs must therefore be included explicitly on both sides of the inequality.

2. The Mills-Graves condition contains the price of new material but not the price of the recycled material. In fact, they are assuming it is free once it is separated and processed. This is technically correct but not very helpful. As sold by a local town, recycled material would practically never be in the form it will be reused in, and it often is not a perfect substitute for the virgin material in any case. The

relevant prices for local officials are the prices of the recycled material itself. (Of course this price reflects, among other things, the further processing necessary, the extent to which it will be substitutable for the virgin material, and the new price, Pm.)

3. The separation costs are significant, not only because they may be substantial monetarily but also because the extent to which residents are willing to take them on will help determine the success of the program. After all, the trash could be separated by attendants at the town's trash collection site, and the quality of the separation (i.e., the lack of contamination by other materials) influences the value of the recycled items. This point suggests breaking separation costs into two terms.

4. In the age of regional trash disposal facilities, the disamenity cost of landfilling is borne in the town where the regional facility exists, and we can assume it has been compensated for it by the charge imposed for disposal in the landfill. Whether it is properly compensated is not relevant for decision makers in other towns, although it is clearly an important larger issue. *Disamenity* is probably not a helpful term to cover what may be unhealthy discharges from the regional facility, the results of which may make the idea of compensation irrelevant.

5. Regardless of whether trash is hauled to a regional landfill or to a regional incinerator with transport costs based on volume, there would almost always be justification for some type of processing to increase the density of the trucked waste (i.e., some type of compaction). There ought to be, therefore, a processing term on the waste side of the expression as well as on the recycling side.

The expression here is a modified version of the Mills-Graves condition to account for points 1 to 5. To determine if an item, i, should be recycled, the following condition must be met:

$$SC(i) + PCR(i) + TCR(i) - PR(i) < PCT(i) + TCT(i) + FT(i), \text{ where:}$$

SC	=	separation costs for recycling
PCR	=	processing costs for recycling
TCR	=	transport costs for recycling
PR	=	price for recycled materials
PCT	=	processing costs for trash
TCT	=	transport costs for trash
FT	=	disposal fee for trash

(PR may be positive or negative)

Obviously, the distribution of separation costs between the households and the attendants at the recycling facility is important. To the extent that households are willing to do the separation and do it so that materials are not contaminated, this will minimize SC from the perspective of the town and reduce the negative component on the left side of the above equation. Mandatory recycling would be helpful because it allows for legal sanctions when there is noncompliance; the passage of a mandatory recycling law may indicate a commitment to recycling in the town.

Even with a strong public acceptance of recycling, some labor cost for monitoring will likely be necessary. It is important to appreciate the fact that some important and potentially recyclable items must be separated by households; the cost of separation once they enter the waste stream is just too high. Examples of this would be almost all the paper products (mixed paper, cardboard, and newspaper), the assortment of organic materials known as yard waste, and household garbage.

On the other hand, there are certain items that require considerable knowledge in order to separate them into appropriate categories for sale. An obvious example is scrap metal. Having it piled in the appropriate grades determines whether it can be sold at a slight profit or whether it will be costly to get rid of. For nonferrous metals (copper, lead, brass, aluminum, etc.) the preceding is also true, but these are generally small items with a generally high value, so these metals are less of a problem. The recycling of glass represents an intermediate case where initial separation can be done in the household, but both the potential for contamination and safety considerations on site suggest that disposal in the bins be done by the attendant(s).

Processing costs for recycling may seem like a minor consideration; just get a few bins and toss the stuff in. In fact, the marketability of separated material is affected markedly by the form it is in. Take cardboard, for example. One would have to pay someone to carry it away in an unprocessed state; if it is baled, and a truckload of bales has accumulated, it will bring $25 per ton on site (in New Hampshire). Plastic jugs, of little value unprocessed due to their low density relative to the high cost of transportation, become a different story when processed. Granulated or baled, their value is in the $0.10 to $0.25 per pound range on site (since they have been made dense enough to overcome the transportation problem). For paper products and plastic appropriate processing is crucial and very likely to prove cost-effective.

Transportation costs for recycled products are closely related to the degree of processing. Transportation costs are often so high that certain separated materials must be processed (particularly to make them more dense) or costs will overwhelm any gains from the sale of the separated material. Items such as aluminum cans are so easy to separate and so high in value (up to $0.35 per pound recently) that transportation costs would rarely affect recycling; the gain would simply be reduced if the cans were transported unprocessed (uncompacted).

Thus the price for recycled products correlates closely with processing. Recent prices in New Hampshire for sorted newspapers, for example, vary from zero at the buyer's site to $25 per ton at a recycling site. Nothing is paid for indeterminant quantities unbaled; the highest price is for a trailer-load, baled, no magazines. Even giving the papers away often justifies recycling given that it could cost $50 to $75 per ton or more to get rid of them in a landfill or at an incinerator. Transportation costs could be the determining factor with unbaled newspapers. Mixed paper, which has a lower value than newspaper, may have to be baled and stored in relatively large amounts to justify recycling. Items such as yard waste, which can be composted on site with little processing, can be given away (PR = 0) cost-effectively as long as the cost of the land used is less than the cost of transportation and landfilling.

Unless both the landfill disposal costs and the transportation costs are expressed in dollars per ton, there is always a significant gain from compaction of trash (i.e., unsorted solid waste). Taken together with the relatively low cost of large-scale compaction, it is reasonable to assume that compacting is always worth doing—there will always be a positive processing cost of trash (PCT > 0). The overall concern with charges for landfilling is filling up the landfill, so charges based on volume are much more likely.

Since we are dealing here with taking the trash someplace else, there will always be transportation costs for trash (i.e., TCT > 0). Given the weight of the containers used for transporting trash and that charges for disposal are usually by volume, commercial trash haulers seem to typically charge by the yard, not by the ton. This, of course, is an additional argument for compaction since it maximizes the tonnage removed per dollar spent on transportation and minimizes temporary trash storage needs on site.

A tipping fee will invariably exist (FT > 0), since in our example the trash that remains after removal of items for recycling must be sent away for disposal. In principle, trash might be purchased at a trash-to-energy plant, but this does not seem to be common, especially given the high cost of disposing of incinerator ash. The disposal fee at trash-to-energy plants seems to be about the same as it is at landfills.

* * *

This cost-benefit approach can be helpful as it allows us a certain perspective on the costs and benefits related to recycling. On the other hand, expressions like the second equation do not take into account the incremental changes that often occur in both costs and benefits as the amount of recycling increases. The related concept of the optimum amount of recycling, as illustrated in Figure 8.1, can best be shown for a number of different items in the waste stream by using the standard tools of microeconomics.

THE MICROECONOMICS OF RECYCLING

One of the disadvantages of the term *recycling* is that it implies somehow that recycling either pays or does not pay. The Mills and Graves condition is very helpful because it correctly suggests an item-by-item analysis to determine whether it pays to recycle any particular item. The materials in

Figure 8.2
Optimal Recycling for Common Materials in the Waste Stream

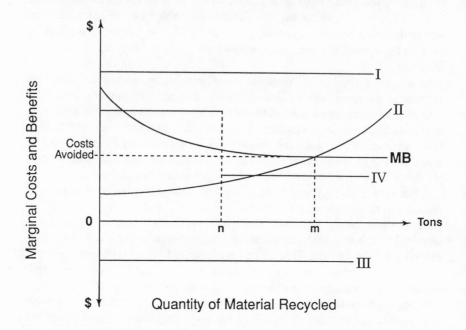

the waste stream are numerous and varied, and their differing market prices, processing requirements, ease of separation and handling, disposal costs, and a number of other factors require that they be dealt with separately. To illustrate the point, and to show how one might apply the tools of microeconomic analysis to individual materials, Figure 8.2 shows how the marginal benefit and marginal cost concepts from Figure 8.1 might be applied to different types of materials.

Marginal Benefits

Some benefits of recycling are unique to certain materials. An obvious example is the revenue from recycling and selling that material. Other benefits are fairly constant (on a per-ton basis) for all materials in the waste stream. Examples are disposal costs avoided and improvement in environmental quality. For simplicity we shall assume in our analysis that benefits refer to the environment independent of the particular material being considered. We will use sale revenue, a benefit unique to each material, as a reduction in costs. This somewhat unusual approach allows us to generate and discuss the helpful idea of a single marginal benefit function for recycling. This could also be thought of as a community demand curve. It would decline

Table 8.1
Willingness to Pay Extra for Recyclable Plastic Containers

Extra Amount ($)	% Willing to Pay
0	42
.01–.05	38
.06–.10	11
.10–.15	9

Source: Society of the Plastics Industry, *Plastics World,* April 1991, p. 21.

because of falling marginal benefits, but would approach a constant value at the dollar value of disposal costs avoided. Presumably the monetary gain from cost avoidance would still be a benefit even if people attached no additional environmental quality benefits to more recycling.

Surveys have been conducted in an attempt to determine the value people place on environmental quality. The results of one such survey are given in Table 8.1. In this case people were asked how much they were willing to pay for a recyclable container. It is possible to estimate the value people place on environmental quality improvements from reduced landfilling by subtracting the expected cost-avoided gain from the charges listed in Table 8.1 for the same volume or weight of containers.

Marginal Costs

The marginal cost of recycling tends to be material-specific. Processing and storage requirements vary greatly. And of course the market price of the recycled materials (included in costs) varies too. With marginal costs being net of these prices, it is possible to identify several distinctive marginal cost patterns and give examples of each. Let us consider four net cost patterns for recycling (net of revenue from the sale of the processed recycled material). One example might be junk furniture or old televisions; the chore of actually disassembling the item is so costly that no amount of recycling is worth doing (i.e., MB < MC at all points). A second possibility would be initally low marginal costs (see Figure 8.1) that justify recycling up to a point, after which the increased marginal costs take over (i.e., MB > MC at low rates but MC > MB at high rates). An example of this might be the range of plastics in the waste stream. At the low recycling cost end, we have the fairly easily recyclable HDPE and PET; at the other end, we have the difficult-to-recycle mixed resin containers and plastics that are part of multimaterial packaging. A third distinct type is a material such as aluminum cans with a high market value that overcomes the separation and processing cost at all recycled amounts (i.e., MB > MC at all points). Last, there is the case in which a particular piece of processing equipment is justified only at large volumes or weights. An example would be cardboard recycling. There are economies of scale for cardboard, so a baler (and the resulting increase in marketability) is justified only if there is adequate volume.

More about the Optimal Amount of Recycling

The preceding discussion on marginal benefits and costs can be presented graphically to identify the optimum amount of recycling for each material. Following a format such as that in Figure 8.1, but using the idea of a constant minimum value for MB at the level of costs avoided, a marginal benefit schedule like that in Figure 8.2 would be appropriate. The four patterns of cost are pictured and numbered from I to IV. I represents difficult items, III is for items with high value, even unprocessed. Note that III is below zero cost. This means that revenue from sale exceeds separation and processing costs. As mentioned, II could represent the different types of plastics, and IV might be cardboard.

The optimal amount for I is zero, for III is "all available," for II is m, and for IV is any amount above n.

Public Benefits, Private Benefits, and Mandatory Recycling

We have noted that the benefits shown in Figure 8.2 are community benefits since trash disposal is usually paid for by tax revenue. On the other hand, individuals can dispose of solid waste at little personal cost, so the cost-avoidance gain is very small. Examples of individual costs are a trip to the dump, a small charge for curbside pickup, or in the old days, a household incinerator. Since individual cost avoidance is low if one recycles, only those with a strong preference for a cleaner environment would recycle. The marginal benefit curves in Figures 8.1 and 8.2 were based on community (as opposed to private) benefits. The distinction between these two types of benefits and how it relates to mandatory recycling is shown in Figure 8.3.

The graphic representation is the same as that in Figure 8.1, except that an individual or private benefit curve has been added and labeled MB_p and the original marginal benefit curve has been relabeled MB_s to stand for marginal social benefit. The point Q still represents the optimal amount of recycling, but the lessser amount Q' would be observed if recycling was voluntary, since individuals have little incentive to consider the (significant) costs avoided benefit. This argument suggests that to achieve the optimal amount of recycling, Q, the recycling program will have to be mandatory.

An alternative way to look at recycling, and one we have mentioned previously, is to consider recycling as a public good with the classic free rider problem. This means that Jones gains the most if everyone else recycles, but Jones does not. In this case Jones would be the free rider. Of course if

Figure 8.3
Individual and Social Benefits from Recycling

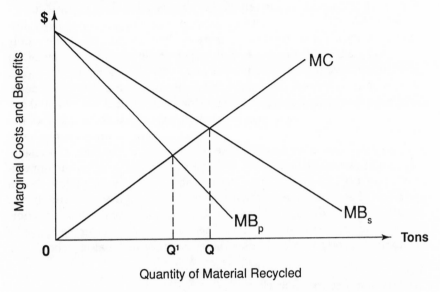

Quantity of Material Recycled

everyone views things the same way, no recycling gets done. Again, this leads us to argue for mandatory recycling.

Estimating the Benefit When the Town Owns a Landfill or Incinerator. One of the advantages when a waste producer has to pay fees to dispose of its waste is that the marginal benefit schedule in Figure 8.1 can be measured explicitly. This is because the cost-avoidance gain from recycling is explicit. A ton removed from the waste stream will have a cost-avoidance gain of X dollars per ton. If a municipality actually owns a landfill or an incinerator, an explicit dollar value for cost avoidance would not be as easy to determine. As shown in Chapter 5, the following gains could be estimated in present value terms: deferring the eventual costs of closing the landfill, deferring the annual disposal costs after the landfill is closed, and reducing annual operating costs for the trash portion of the solid waste stream.

Separation Costs. Solid waste planners and other managers in different institutional settings generally ignore separation costs in doing cost-benefit analyses for recycling. They may distribute information or containers to assist in this task, but the daily separating is viewed as free. At the practical level this could become a problem. Recycling programs ought to focus initially on those items that are easiest to separate. Those are the ones with the lowest private costs. Whether the program is voluntary or mandatory, officials could train separators in these easy items without dumping major separation tasks on them all at once.

More about Processing. Once materials have been separated, the single most important determinant of marketability of recyclables is processing. We are talking almost exclusively about materials that have a low value-to-volume ratio. Since transportation costs can easily negate this (low) value, recycled materials are processed to increase their density. Most commonly this is done either by baling, as with paper products and scrap metal, or granulating/shredding, as with plastics and (sometimes) scrap metal. Proper processing often permits the items to be sold or given away at the dock. Otherwise they must be carted elsewhere or disposed of at a substantial fee. A discussion of processing again makes the point that recycling does not produce just one product. In fact it produces a whole array of products, each of which may have its own scale requirements for efficient processing. Aluminum cans will be picked up by buyers at modest volumes and unprocessed, whereas scrap metal often must be accumulated to large volumes (in the range of several hundred tons) in order to be sold from one site. Figure 8.1 uses corrugated cardboard to show the cost impact of reaching a volume that justifies the purchase of a baler. This is obviously an example of a scale economy of production and raises the question of regional recycling.

Costs and Regional Recycling

It may be the case that the volume of material needed to justify the purchase of a particular piece of equipment is available, but that storage requirements for successful marketing require a much larger enclosure. In this case, processing could take place at several locations, and storage and marketing could be centralized in a regional facility. The general rule of thumb would be to decentralize processing as much as possible to minimize the significant transportation costs associated with carrying separated but unprocessed material over great distances. A regional solid waste plan, using recycling as a key component, would likely generate various sized recycling facilities throughout the region to account for the differing scale requirements of collection, processing, storage, and marketing. Local trash officials may consider it less expensive to have private residents or commercial haulers carry separated but unprocessed materials considerable distances to a single regional facility, but this simply shifts the costs to the private sector. If the economics of the situation justify different levels of facilities, the overall cost to society would be minimized by having such diversified facilities and paying for them with public funds.

Materials with Adverse Environmental Effects

Certain materials are separated out of the waste stream, not primarily because they are reusable (although they might be) but because they cannot

Figure 8.4
The Benefit of Recycling for Difficult (Type I) Materials

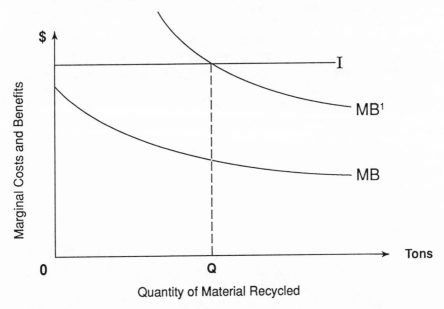

Quantity of Material Recycled

be landfilled and/or incinerated. Examples are demolition waste, tires, appliances (white goods), junk furniture, and automotive waste liquids. Such materials often require disposal systems that tend to be costly. However, they tend to have adverse effects if thrown away. Roadside, vacant lot, or out-of-the-way dumping of such materials can have significant negative environmental effects. These are often visual, but may also involve contamination of water or soil. Such materials would have marginal cost schedules like I in Figure 8.2. A problem arises if an item cannot be disposed of as trash, yet is not worth recycling. The benefits of recycling include environmental improvements, so it seems reasonable that the MB schedule for recycling these materials might be well above that for other materials, as shown in Figure 8.2. To show this, we redraw the relevant facts from 8.2 as Figure 8.4. MB' shows the true benefit from returning these materials, and we now see that the optimum recycling rate can be greater than zero, even if the materials are costly to dispose of. It is simply a question of the proper accounting of the benefits of recycling.

At the practical level, individuals bringing such materials often have to pay a fee. It must be high enough to cover all or most of the external disposal fee, but low enough so it does not induce people to dump the item in a convenient spot.

SUMMARY

The recycling of solid wastes is an excellent example in applied microeconomics. The market failure known as the *negative externality* can be illustrated with clarity, using as an example solid waste disposal costs. The concepts familiar to the student of microeconomics, that is, public goods, economies of scale, optimality, and fixed proportions, were discussed in Chapter 8.

Of further interest to students of microeconomics is whether recycling and other waste disposal methods are complementary. Chapter 9 discusses this issue and others.

9

Larger Issues: Integrated Waste Management, Reduction and Reuse, and the Throw-Away Lifestyle

It has not been the purpose of this book to address all the issues and problems related to solid waste management. The focus has been on one particular management technique, recycling. It has been shown that, if the disposal problem is approached systematically and if all the benefits of recycling are accounted for, recycling is often cost-effective. Among the issues not considered in detail here were (1) the efficacy of integrated waste management, (2) the 3Rs movement, and (3) the question of whether recycling is a real reform. These larger issues are considered in Chapter 9.

INTEGRATED WASTE MANAGEMENT

A term in common use now in solid waste management circles is *integrated waste management*. Although often defined as a program meant to integrate incineration and recycling, it can also mean the integration of recycling with either landfilling or comprehensive composting.

It should be noted that up to 20 percent of the waste stream presents significant problems for any conventional trash disposal methods. Materials such as hazardous waste (industrial or household), junk appliances and junk furniture, tires, demolition waste including shingles, and many different wheeled vehicles cannot be dealt with except in specialized facilities. Recycling offers at least some answers, as renovation or repair and reuse is possible with items such as used bicycles, old furniture, wood from demolitions, used recreation equipment, and so on. Most of this stuff cannot be incinerated, landfilled, or composted.

Incineration and Recycling

Although integrated waste management has a nice ring to it and sounds like rational planning, it is quite misleading. The term *integrated* implies that things fit together. In the case of recycling and incineration, it would imply that they were somehow complementary. In fact they are not at all complementary and in many cases represent alternatives for waste disposal. Those items that provide most of the BTUs in a trash-burning plant are often those that can be recycled. The most obvious examples are the plastics, but yard waste and most paper burn well but are recyclable. Even if a modest fee has to be paid to a recycled paper broker to remove low end (mainly mixed) paper, the cost is still likely to be far less than the $50 or $70 or $100 per ton paid to get rid of it at the trash-to-energy plant. Other recyclables such as aluminum, other metals, and glass of course are not wanted at the incinerator. Food waste contains BTUs, but generally has a high water content and is far from being first choice as a fuel. However, it can be composted very successfully with yard waste.

It is easy to get caught up in the apparent simplicity of a trash-to-energy plant—plastics, paper, and yard waste should be burned, and aluminum and glass should be recycled. As shown here, however, proper cost accounting gives a quite different result, one that allows little space for incineration in solid waste planning.

Two additional notes on the economics of incineration seem appropriate. The first has to do with the large-scale technology required in trash-to-energy plants. The operators of such plants require a large, dependable flow of mostly burnable trash. They therefore have a strong incentive to sign contracts that require a minimum amount of trash from each trash producer. This of course implies a minimum payment. If a recycling program is successful and a trash producer's supply of burnables falls below the minimum, the payment still must be made. This of course will reduce the incentive to recycle. What all of this suggests is that recycling and incineration are substitutes, not complements, and so it is totally inappropriate to present them as two parts of integrated waste management. Contracts that require a certain payment even if the amount of trash becomes very small are called *put or pay* and should be avoided.

An additional problem with incineration should be mentioned. A trash incinerator does not really get rid of materials. The best it can do is reduce the volume and weight. The materials are converted to ash (assuming that air pollution control devices minimize air emissions), which tends to be quite toxic. Disposal of this ash is a problem and must be done carefully and in special landfills. Most of the trash is simply densified in an incinerator.

Composting and Recycling

One must be careful when using the term *composting*. Three levels of composting can be identified, and each has different implications for recycling and trash disposal. The simplest type of composting involves the dumping of yard waste (and chipped wood and brush, if available) in a pile and letting it rot (compost) until it is useful as mulch or soil enhancer. This process can be accelerated and the final product improved by turning it over, adding lime, using a commercial composter, and so on, but it is basically simple and the typical way in which yard waste and/or clean wood are dealt with in a recycling program. It is, in other words, complementary to recycling.

The next level of composting involves the addition of food waste to the mixture. This again is complementary to recycling, although more attention must be paid to the process since problems with odor, rodents, and scavaging mammals (including bears in some places) exist to a much greater degree than they do with yard waste composting. Even though it is a somewhat more complicated process than composting yard waste, the addition of food waste to a composting program still is complementary to recycling and often an integral part of such a program.

The last and by far most complex composting program involves all organic waste. This primarily means the addition of just about all paper products to the recycling program. Since these paper products can account for 40 percent or more of household, office, or retail waste, we are talking a quantum increase in material. Such composting programs are recent and continue to be controversial. There are two reasons for concern with this technology. The first involves questions about the toxicity of the resulting compost. Once one moves past #1 newspaper (no glossies), "paper" contains a fair amount of toxic dyes and various other additives. The resulting compost, although claimed safe by the sellers of this technology, has raised questions among environmental chemists and others. The second problem with large-scale composting involves the issue of whether composting at this level is complementary to recycling. In principle it probably is, since the resulting material (at least according to some) can be incorporated safely in the soil. From a monetary perspective, however, such large-scale composting is far from cost-effective. Since the cost of running these complex composting operations is about the same as incineration or landfilling, they represent a far more costly disposal method than recycling. The cost-avoidance gain from recycling even low value newspaper and mixed paper is achieved when they are recycled, not composted. Recycling paper instead of composting it is probably a better deal by anywhere from $25 to $100 a ton, depending on the type of paper. It is difficult, in other words, to make much of an economic argument on behalf of large-scale composting instead of recycling. Once paper is added, recycling and composting are substitutes, not complements, and hence *integrated waste management* is also a misleading term in the case of comprehensive composting.

Landfilling and Recycling

With the exception of hazardous waste and problem items that cannot be handled in conventional incineration or composting and are a challenge for recycling, basically all waste is acceptable in a modern, lined landfill (or even in many older landfills or dumps). Because it is comprehensive in a sense, landfilling is a different kind of trash disposal system. Neither incineration nor large-scale composting would be called comprehensive. An interesting implication of this is that landfilling is the only trash disposal system that is complementary to recycling. Our purpose is not to push landfilling, and we have shown that recycling should be the first choice for solid waste management (actually, the 3Rs — source reduction, reuse, and recycling). However, after all intensive efforts toward the 3Rs are accomplished, and the author has argued that this could take care of the vast majority of common household waste, the only thing left for the remainder is landfilling. (Note: In areas of large populations and hence large initial amounts of solid waste, there may be sufficient leftovers after recycling for a carefully designed trash-to-energy plant. Also, there may be safer ways than landfilling for long-term trash storage, since that's all that landfilling is.) An example would be to use this trash, after intense compaction, as the inner material in various types of concrete construction in power plants for example. This is being done in certain countries.

REDUCTION AND REUSE

In recent years there has been a movement among environmental groups to take a more global/systems view of economizing on resources than that provided by recycling alone. This approach is most commonly called the 3Rs — reduction, reuse, and recycling. Since recycling has been covered in depth here, we will focus on reduction and reuse.

Reduction

Reduction, or more properly *source reduction*, would cover such changes as (1) an absolute reduction in the amount of packaging used, (2) an increase in the use of single material packaging, and (3) an increase in the use of materials that are recyclable, or better yet, returnable. Examples of excess packaging are easy to find. How many millions of people every day have to wrestle with the several layers of plastic that now cover many products? The arguments about security, ease of shipping, or whatever to try to justify all this packaging are difficult to take seriously. The amount of packaging is often far in excess of an amount that would be used if the true waste disposal cost had to be extracted from company profits.

In this throw-away society, major efforts at source reduction are difficult to initiate at the local level. Certainly organizing around so-called bottle bills is very helpful. This gives people an incentive to return the containers for materials recovery and reuse, thus reducing the use of virgin materials. Several states are considering bills restricting in different ways the use of certain material combinations. Examples include taxes on multimetal cans and banning disposable diapers. Stores have begun to offer produce and dry goods in bulk. Citizen groups should encourage stores to expand bulk buying and educate people about how to buy in bulk. Realistically, there are serious lifestyle problems here, as we have become used to perfect products (or at least perfect-looking products). Legislative initiatives are likely to have more impact in the area of source reduction than they are with regard to recycling; perhaps that is why local groups tend to focus their efforts on the latter. Visible success with recycling can be achieved with little or no external funding or legislation.

Reuse

The terms *source reduction* and *reuse* sometimes get a little confusing. After all, don't bottle bills, for example, encourage people to turn the bottles back in so that the material can be reused? Yet bottle bills are listed here as source reduction. Although quite arbitrary, a common distinction between reuse and source reduction is that *reuse* refers to using the material again without significant processing. Using this definition, bottle deposits on throw-away containers would lead to source reduction, and bottle deposits on returnables would encourage reuse since the container itself is reused. The material in disposable containers must be processed before being used again.

Perhaps the easiest type of reuse of materials or items from the solid waste stream occurs at the point at which the trash is generated. Examples in the office include the repeated reuse for internal mail of envelopes received from the outside; examples in warehouses and department stores would include the reuse of cardboard boxes and in residential areas the passing around of baby clothes in the neighborhood. Of course, these are just a very few examples, with the possibilities limited only by the imagination of the trash producer.

A second level at which reuse can be facilitated is through some type of swap shop or thrift shop at a recycling facility. This is an excellent location for volunteers, with such operations sometimes run totally by some club or other organization. It could be a local church providing used clothing and household goods out of a store front, a traditional project for classes in school looking to raise money for a class trip, or maybe the Lion's Club doing its part for the environment in the community. Whatever the mechanism, the reuse of separated goods is an excellent device for reducing trash as the reused item replaces one that would have been purchased (and then thrown away). Of course by not throwing the item away, trash disposal costs are avoided.

Examples of reuse would include, but are in no way limited to:

- making home compost piles. (See Appendix 2.3 for more information.)
- used clothing, toys, household goods, and so on, provided to local charities, siblings, people in the neighborhood, and so forth.
- giving egg cartons, coffee cans, baby food jars, and the like to day care centers and schools.
- using old tires in playgrounds.
- using plastic containers with covers for food storage, separating materials in the workshop, holding small toys, in lunch boxes, and at the desk (imagine how many paper clip holders are needed in a major insurance office or in a university.
- fixing up and reusing toys at Christmas (by the police or fire department), or sending bicycles to the Third World (by an organization called Bikes Not Bombs).
- passing along containers that plants come in so that they can be used by others, including the local greenhouse.
- disassembling appliances and various wheeled vehicles so the parts can be reused (a friend has brought to the attention of the author BMW's reverse assembly plant in Germany where old BMWs are totally disassembled for parts renovation and reuse).

A Final Note

As a number of social critics have pointed out to the author, effort spent on recycling programs obscures the real roots of the solid waste crisis. Among these are at least the following: (1) the mentality of the throw-away society, (2) the never-ending drive to consume in the United States and in the rest of the industrialized world, and (3) the way in which the market is unable to incorporate trash disposal costs in market prices (what economists call *market failure*). I stand guilty as charged. My defense is to think globally, act locally. Starting at the local level with recycling programs seems to not only provide for a cleaner local environment, but could educate people on the larger issues. These same people might begin to change their views of consumption and work at getting others to do likewise. Perhaps at some point in the future, the conservation ethic will replace the consumption ethic and the throw-away society will become a historical footnote.

Postscript: RECYCLE Your Anger and Frustration

Late last summer, West Chesterfield and the surrounding towns announced the addition of tin cans to their recycling program. Dog food, cat food, coffee, soup, and fruit cans were to be separated, rinsed, and flattened. Oh, no, I thought, another chore to add to my list! Me with my pair of Siberian Huskies and their three pups! Yuk! Grudgingly, I saved my rinsed fourteen-plus dog food cans per week in separate brown grocery bags . . . and grudgingly watched them pile up.

My procrastination lasted about six weeks until one Friday night when I decided to tackle those cans. All the bottoms had to be removed before the cans could be squashed. After flattening five or six, I noticed that it sort of felt good. Maybe this chore could be fun! The vigorous stomping of a few more cans found me shouting, "Here take that, you miserable so and so!" Eventually this led to humanizing the cans by giving them names of people I was angry or frustrated with. (Some people or companies need more crushing, flattening, and harder stomping on than others, depending on the anger/ frustration level.)

Too soon the task was over . . . I couldn't wait until the next batch was ready. In the meantime, I could be mentally creating my new list of people who need flattening . . . didn't I miss a couple the first time? Yes, recycling can be fun! Recycle! It's good for you!

Brenda Phillips, 1991

Appendixes

Appendix 1.1

GLOSSARY OF TERMS

Avoided Costs. Certain solid waste management costs, such as tipping fees or landfill/incineration costs, which may not be incurred due to a recycling program.

Biodegradable. The property of a substance that permits it to be broken down by micro-organisms into simple, stable compounds such as carbon dioxide and water.

Capital Costs. Costs involved in beginning or upgrading a solid waste management program, e.g., equipment, buildings, storage bins, vehicles, etc.

Container Deposit Law. A law requiring deposits on beverage containers, such as glass bottles, aluminum cans and plastic containers. Deposits are redeemed by the consumer when containers are returned to a redemption center.

Composting. A method of waste management in which a targeted part of the organic fraction of the solid waste stream is biologically decomposed under controlled conditions of oxygen, moisture and temperature. The end product is a stable, soil-like substance that can be easily and safely handled and applied to the land.

Corrugated. To be bent into a series of folds or alternate ridges and furrows, as in corrugated cardboard.

Demolition Debris. Waste materials produced through demolition processes, such as demolished buildings, roads or bridges.

Energy Recovery. The generation of energy by burning solid waste; also, the generation of energy by capturing methane gas from garbage decomposition in a landfill.

Ferrous Metal. Metal which contains iron; will be drawn to a magnet. (See *nonferrous*.)

Gaylord Box. Standard, triple-wall corrugated container often used to store and transport recyclable materials.

Hazardous Waste. A substance considered hazardous because it contains one or more of these characteristics; it is flammable, reactive or explosive when mixed with other substances, or is corrosive or toxic. These wastes require special disposal because they are harmful to humans or the natural environment.

HDPE. A type of plastic made from high-density polyethylene resins. Includes such plastics as milk and water jugs, and non-food plastic containers, such as laundry detergent bottles, antifreeze and lubricating oil bottles and dishwashing liquid bottles.

Incineration. Process of burning solid waste, with or without energy recovery, for volume reduction.

Landfill. A site for the controlled burial of solid waste.

Leachate. Liquid produced by a mixture of solid waste decomposition and water flowing through the top surface of a landfill or dump, containing dissolved or suspended materials. May contaminate groundwater or surface water if it drains from the bottom or sides of the landfill or dump.

Methane. A colorless, odorless, flammable, potentially dangerous gaseous hydrocarbon (present in natural gas) formed by the decomposition of organic matter. Can be recovered from landfills and used as a fuel.

Natural Resource. Valuable, naturally occurring material such as wood, minerals, water or crude oil.

Nonferrous Metal. Metal containing little or no iron; will not be drawn to a magnet. (See *ferrous.*)

Nonrenewable Resource. A natural resource that, because of its scarcity, the great length of time it takes to form or its rapid depletion, is considered limited in amount, such as copper, tin, crude oil and bauxite.

OCC. Old corrugated containers.

Operating and Maintenance Costs. Recurring program costs necessary to manage and maintain a solid waste program.

PET. A type of plastic made from polyethylene terephthalate resins, used primarily as soda bottle containers.

Raw Material. Unprocessed natural resource or product used in a manufacturing process.

Recyclable. A product that contains resources which have the potential to be recycled.

Recycle. A process whereby any product or material which has served its intended end-use and which has been separated from solid waste is remanufactured into a usable product, either in the same form or as part of a different product.

Renewable Resource. A natural resource derived from an endless or cyclical source, such as wood, water and plants.

Reuse. To extend the life of an item by using it again, repairing it, modifying it or creating new uses for it.

Sludge. The by-product of a wastewater treatment plant.

Solid Waste. All solid and semi-solid materials generated for disposal, including household discards, yard waste, commercial discards, industrial wastes, sludge, demolition and construction wastes and ashes.

Solid Waste Management. The process of controlling, handling and disposal of all solid waste.

Tipping Fee. The amount of money paid to dispose, or "tip," solid waste in a disposal facility, usually expressed in tons or cubic yards.

Waste Reduction. To decrease the amount of solid waste generated by households, businesses and industries.

Waste Stream. Composition of materials in solid waste, generally discussed in terms of tonnage or cubic yards.

Source: New Hampshire Resource Recovery Association, *Recycling in New Hampshire,* 1988, pp. iii–iv.

Appendix 1.2

SOLID WASTE MANAGEMENT JOURNALS

Biocycle, JG Press, Inc., 419 State Ave., Emmaus, Pa. 18049. (215) 967-4135; $58 per year, published 12 times per year.

Management of World Wastes, 6255 Barfield Road, Atlanta, Ga. 30328. (404) 256-9800; $45 per year, published 12 times per year.

Public Works, Public Works Journal Corp., 200 S. Broad St., Ridgewood, N.J. 07451. (201) 445-5800; $30 per year, published 12 times per year.

Recycling Today, GIE Publishers, 4012 Bridge Ave., Cleveland, Ohio 44113. (216) 961-4130; $28 per year, published monthly.

Resource Recycling, P.O. Box 10540, Portland, Oregon 97210. (503) 227-1319; FAX 503-227-3613; $42 per year, published 12 times per year.

Scrap Processing and Recycling, 1325 G Street N.W., Suite 1000, Washington, D.C. 20006. (202) 466-4050; $26 per year, published bimonthly.

Waste Age, 1730 Rhode Island Ave. N.W., Suite 1000, Washington, D.C. 20036. (202) 654-4613; $45 per year, published monthly.

Source: New Hampshire Resource Recovery Association, *Recycling in New Hampshire*, 1988, p. 155 (updated 1992).

Appendix 1.3

TRADE ASSOCIATIONS

The Aluminum Association, 900 19th St. N.W., Suite 300, Washington, D.C. 20006. (202) 862–5100; aluminum can recycling.

American Paper Institute/Paper Recycling Committee, 260 Madison Ave., New York, N.Y. 10016. (212) 340–0600; paper recycling.

Glass Packaging Institute, 1801 K St., N.W., Suite 1100SL, Washington, D.C. 20036. (202) 887–4850; glass recycling.

Institute of Scrap Recycling Industries, 1627 K St. N.W., Suite 700, Washington, D.C. 20006. (202) 466–4050; metals, paper, plastic, and textile recycling.

Society of the Plastics Industry, 1275 K St. N.W., Suite 300, Washington, D.C. 20005. (202) 371–5200; plastic recycling.

Source: NHRRA, 1988, p. 153 (updated 1992).

Appendix 2.1A

SIGN IN A WHITE PAPER RECYCLING PROGRAM

WHITE PAPER

ACCEPTED

White Notebook Paper
White Laser Print Paper
White Letterhead Paper
White Envelopes (plastic and wax paper windows MUST be removed)

NOT ACCEPTED

Please place these items in the trash.

Overnight/Express Envelopes
Carbon Paper
Trash (plastic, metal bindings, candy wrappers, etc.)

PLEASE NOTE

* Color Print on White Paper is Accepted
* Please Place White Glossy Paper and White Triplicate (NCR) Forms with Mixed Paper.
* Staples are OK

Printed on Recycled Paper

For questions or assistance call campus extension 2567

Source: Keene State College, Keene, N.H., 1991.

Appendix 2.1B

SIGN IN A MIXED PAPER RECYCLING PROGRAM

MIXED PAPER

 ACCEPTED

White Glossy Paper, Colored Paper, Magazines,
Catalogs, Telephone Books, File Folders, Manilla
Envelopes, Books (please remove hard covers),
Colored Envelopes (plastic and wax paper windows
MUST be removed), Brown "Ground Wood" Computer
Paper, and Triplicate (NCR) Forms

NOT ACCEPTED

Please place these items in the trash.
Paperboard (6-pack holders, cereal or
tissue boxes, etc.) and Carbon Paper
Overnight/Express Envelopes
Trash (plastic or metal bindings, candy
wrappers, etc.)

PLEASE NOTE

* Please Place White Paper Separately
* Please Place Brown Paper Bags With Cardboard
* Staples are OK

Printed on Recycled Paper

For questions or assistance
call campus extension 2567

Source: Keene State College, Keene, N.H., 1991.

140

Appendix 2.2

FLOW CHART FOR COMPREHENSIVE COMPOSTING

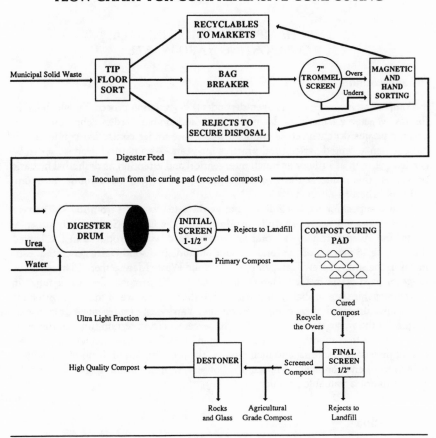

Source: Lawrence W. King, "A Technical Study of Municipal Solid Waste Composting and the Effect of Disposable Paper Diapers," Cincinnati, Ohio: Procter & Gamble, 1991, p. 2.

141

Appendix 2.3

NEW HAMPSHIRE GUIDELINES FOR
COMPOSTING YARD WASTE

Background

Composting is an aerobic (oxygen-dependent) degradation process by which plants (leaves, vegetable trimmings, lawn clippings, and similar garden debris) and other organic wastes (kitchen refuse, sludge) decompose under controlled conditions. It has been an accepted agricultural practice for years. As a natural process, it can be carried out with as little or as much intervention and attention as desired. The basic parameters that influence the composting process are oxygen, temperature, moisture, and the carbon-to-nitrogen ratio (C:N).

Waste composition studies indicate that yard waste represents from 10 to 30 percent of municipal solid waste. A study conducted for the United States Environmental Protection Agency found the total amount of yard waste produced in the United States to be 18 percent of the total amount of municipal solid waste generated. Estimates in the state of New Hampshire's 1988 Solid Waste Management Plan show the range of yard waste in New Hampshire to be 2 to 18 percent. The lower range in New Hampshire can probably be attributed to the rural nature of the state with most yard waste disposed of or composted on site. Yard waste represents a greater percentage of the waste stream (from 35 to 40 percent) during certain times of the year.

A yard waste composting program has many benefits. These include the avoided cost of disposal at landfills and incinerators, the preservation of disposal capacity, a reduction of environmental impact, the conservation of natural resources, and the production of a valuable product.

Legislation

During the 1989 legislative session, composting was a component of two bills that were passed. In House Bill 289, *compost* was formally defined as "plant debris from yard waste including tree, shrub, and grass clippings which is arranged in a way that encourages rapid conversion, decay, and decomposition by alternating layers of the plant debris with animal manure and soil or layers of plant debris with layers of chemical fertilizer and soil. Compost is a stable, soil-like substance which can be beneficially used and which must be of the quality to be easily and safely handled, stored and applied to the land." This bill also authorized and encouraged towns and counties to create and use compost and woodchips in parks and highways and to sell or freely distribute municipally created compost and wood chips to residents. Senate Bill 156 allowed composting as a means of weight reduction to meet the requirements established in the same bill.

Establishing a Municipal Composting Program

When planning a yard waste composting program the following areas need to be addressed: quantity of material, material collection, facility siting, equipment, staffing, public education, and marketing/end use.

1. *Quantity of Material.* Determining the amount of yard waste that will be available can be done by using established generation rates or actual weight studies. Since yard waste does not occur at a constant rate throughout the year, care must be taken in the analysis of collected data. In most cases, existing generation rates should be adequate.

2. *Material Collection.* Collection of yard wastes for a municipal program can be separated into three categories: drop-off, curbside pickup in bags or other containers, or bulk pickup where the leaves are collected loose off the street. If bags are to be used for collection, they should be biodegradable. This type of bag can be shredded and mixed into the compost while nondegradable plastic bags must be removed before composting. Bulk collection requires that the material be scooped, raked, swept, or vacuumed off the street. Vacuuming of leaves is slower, and care must be exercised to prevent contaminants that may exist in the street from being mixed in with the yard waste. This method of collection may clog storm sewers and can be a fire hazard. The choice of collection methods should be determined by cost, convenience, household participation rate, and the amount and type of yard waste to be collected.

3. *Facility Siting.* Land requirement will be dependent on the volume of yard waste to be collected and the level of technology to be employed. As the level of technology increases, the amount of land required for processing decreases. In general, one acre of land can support 4,000 to 6,000 cubic yards of loose material. Criteria to be considered for a composting site are location, size, accessibility, soil drainage, surface water, topography, buffers, and security. It is important that the site be of adequate size to handle all current and future material that will be received at the facility.

4. *Equipment.* Equipment for a composting program must be able to handle movement, turning, watering, screening, and monitoring of the material. Specialized equipment is available for collection and windrow turning, but is not necessary. The use of a screen does, however, create material of uniform size, which helps in the marketing of the end product but is not necessary.

5. *Staffing.* A staff that is dedicated and understands the material and the composting process is needed to ensure a successful program. Of the staff's responsibilities, the areas of windrow monitoring, recordkeeping, and quality control are the most important.

6. *Public Education.* Education has become a vital component of any successful recycling program. Education and promotional programs should start as soon as the planning process is

initiated. The information should answer these basic questions: why, how, what, when, and where. Information can be distributed in a number of different ways, each targeting a different audience. Education should not stop once the program has started, but be a continuous process with updates and reminders to maintain interest and participation.

7. *Marketing/End Use.* There are a number of uses for compost. As a soil amendment, it improves the texture, porosity, and water-holding capacity; it also increases the organic content of the soil. For mulch, it is placed around plants to suppress weeds, modify soil temperature, and conserve soil moisture. On slopes, it can be used for stabilization and reducing erosion. In a greenhouse or nursery, it can be used as one of the components of a potting soil mix.

The product can be given away, sold, or traded to residents, landscapers, nurseries, greenhouses, and local governments. It is usually distributed in bulk with pickup at the composting site by the user. As with any product, the higher the quality, the easier it is to market. Nursery owners and landscapers are more apt to reject a product with extraneous material in it, so if they are to be a major outlet for the compost, they should be contacted in the planning stages to ensure that an acceptable product is produced.

Composting by Windrows

Processing of compost in windrows (long narrow piles similar to those cut in hay fields prior to baling) can range from a low level of technology to a highly sophisticated system. As the technology increases, labor and equipment requirements also increase. As a trade-off, the higher levels of technology require less land and the breakdown of the material occurs at a more rapid rate. A low level of technology may be most adaptable for New Hampshire communities. For this technology, material is placed in windrows and turned every four to eight weeks with a frontend loader. A marketable product is obtained in ten to twelve months.

The general concept behind the processing of yard waste is the formation of a windrow or pile so that the proper biological conditions are created.

Naturally occurring microorganisms found in the yard wastes and soil break a windrow down into friable material. There are two major categories of microorganisms in an aerobic composting process. Mesophilic organisms are active at temperatures above freezing and their activity causes temperatures within the windrow to increase. At temperatures above 110°F, thermophilic organisms become active and decomposition increases. Above 140°F, these aerobic, oxygen-loving organisms begin to die and decomposition decreases. These organisms are dependent on oxygen, temperature, moisture, and the proper carbon-to-nitrogen (C:N) ratio to carry out this natural process. The optimum level of oxygen for aerobic organisms to effectively break down leaf and yard waste is 5 percent. Levels below this result in the organisms' dying off and less efficient decomposition by anaerobic organisms.

As indicated, the temperature in the compost pile should be between 100 and 140 degrees Fahrenheit. It is the natural digestion process by organisms that results in increased temperatures within the compost. If properly constructed, the temperature in a windrow will be self-sustaining until the compost is stabilized.

A moisture content of 40 to 60 percent by weight is optimal. This will be the consistency of a wrung-out sponge. Moisture is necessary to dissolve nutrients for use as a food source by the microorganisms. Excessive moisture creates an undesirable anaerobic condition. Water may need to be added when the windrows are initially formed, and turned, to maintain the proper moisture content.

A C:N ratio of 20:1 to 30:1 is ideal. Leaves tend to have a C:N ratio of 60:1 to 80:1, which results in slower decomposition. Materials high in nitrogen can be added to improve the ratio.

The windrow or pile is then turned to maintain these conditions and speed decomposition. Turning the windrow can be done as little as once a year to as frequently as once a week. It should be noted that the less frequently a compost pile is turned, the greater the problem of odors, due to the anaerobic state that exists within the pile.

Additional steps can be added before and after windrow formation. Preprocessing may involve removal of unwanted material and conditioning of the waste by grinding, shredding, wetting, and/or mixing. Post-processing is shredding and/or screening as an additional means to remove unwanted material plus preparing a product for distribution. These additional steps will cut the composting time, reduce the volume, and improve the quality of the end product. The time frame for a stable marketable product will range from a few months to three years or more, depending upon the climate as well as the frequency of turning.

A finished product can be determined by two methods. The first method is to place a sample in a plastic bag for 24 to 28 hours at room temperature. If there is no significant odor on opening the bag after this time, the process is complete. The second method monitors temperature or odor. If there is no odor, or the temperature in the windrow does not increase seven days after turning, the compost can be considered stable. It may be desirable to test the quality of the finished product to determine its value and whether market standards are met.

Cost-Benefit Analysis

No program should be started without a feasibility study. For a composting program, this should encompass reviewing the amount of material recovered, capital/ start-up costs, operating and maintenance costs, avoided disposal and transport costs/revenues, and the net program cost/revenue. Each item should be reviewed in detail to make a responsible decision. In the publication "Yard Waste Composting, A Study of Eight Programs" put out by the United States Environmental Protection Agency, the cost of composting ranged from $11 to $102 per ton and the avoided landfill disposal fees ranged from $5 to $137 per ton. The wide range stresses the need for each individual program to be looked at on a case-by-case basis.

Backyard Composting

Composting in the backyard involves the same basic principles as with a municipal program, except on a much smaller scale. Additional organic materials (garden and kitchen waste) can be added without creating additional effort. Although a compost pile can be constructed on open ground, special structures can be purchased or made to save space and hasten the decomposition process.

Conclusion

Composting is a cost-effective means of dealing with the organic section of the municipal solid waste stream and an essential part of an integrated solid waste management plan.

Appendix 2.4

END-USE MARKETS FOR CONSTRUCTION
AND DEMOLITION WASTE

Waste Type	End-Use
Asphalt	
From repairing roads and shingles	Mixed with recyclable asphalt for road and bridge resurfacing
Concrete	Fill, Roadbed
Metal	
Aluminum	"The gold of C&D," remelted
Appliances/White Goods	Scrap metal dealers for crushing
Brass	Scrap metal dealers
Copper	"The other gold of C&D," remelted/reused
Ferrous Pipes, Roofing, Flashing, etc.	Scrap metal dealers
Steel	Scrap metal dealers
Wood	
Untreated	Chipped for fuel, Landscaping, Compost bulking, Animal bedding, Manufactured building products
Treated	May or may not be chipped for fuel, Landscaping, Compost bulking, Animal bedding. Manufactured building products (depending on environmental regulations that vary among states)

Waste Type	End-Use
Other Mixed C&D Waste	
Brick	Masonry, Landscaping, Ornamental stone
Fiberglass	None known
Glass	Recycled into fiberglass insulation, Salvaged
Gypsum/Sheetrock	Chipped into raw material, Soil amendment
Plastic	Chipped/Shredded and used to make insulation
Porcelain	Reused, if in good condition, ground and mixed with concrete
Topsoil	Soil, Soil conditioner, Landscaping, Landfill cover
Used Corrugated Cardboard	Fuel pellets, recycled into new cardboard
Miscellaneous Waste	
Carpet	None known
Fuel Storage Tanks	Can be recycled, once cleaned
Linoleum	None known
Other Unspecified Waste	Markets vary

Source: Robert Spencer, "Taking Control of C&D Debris," *Biocycle*, July 1991, p. 66.

Appendix 3.1

SELECTED LOCATIONS OF
MATERIALS RECOVERY FACILITIES (MRFs)

A selection of operational materials recovery facilities (MRFs) in the United States, including at least one from each of the twenty-eight states having an operational MRF.

STATE	LOCATION	OPERATOR	THROUGHPUT (TPD)
Alabama	Montgomery	McGinnis Ctr.	10 (a)
Arizona	Phoenix	City of Phoenix	20 (a)
California	Anaheim	Taormina Industries	300 (a)
California	Fresno	WMI	200 (d)
California	San Francisco	Norcal	185 (a); 200 (d)
Connecticut	Danbury	RTI	90 (d)
Florida	Jacksonville	BFI	100 (d)
Florida	Orlando	WMI of Florida	85 (a); 300 (d)
Florida	West Palm Beach	Palm Beach County SWA	220 (d)
Georgia	Atlanta	Recycle America – WMI	100 (d)
Illinois	McCook	Waste Watchers/ Crown Disposal	25 (d)
Illinois	Wheeling	Buffalo Grove/ Wheeling Disposal-WMI	10 (a); 15 (d)
Iowa	Carroll	Carroll County SWMC	7 (a); 30 (d)
Louisiana	Baton Rouge	City of Baton Rouge	50 (a); 150 (d)

STATE	LOCATION	OPERATOR	THROUGHPUT (TPD)
Maine	Bowdoinham	Town of Bowdoinham	5 (a)
Maryland	Finksburg	Phoenix Recycling	100 (a); 300 (d)
Massachusetts	Springfield	Resource Recovery Systems	210 (a); 240 (d)
Michigan	Ann Arbor	City of Ann Arbor	100 (d)
Minnesota	St. Louis Park	WMI	90 (a); 150 (d)
New Hampshire	Hookset	Resource Conservation Services	100 (d)
New Jersey	Newark	REI	200 (a); 500 (d)
New Jersey	Woodbine	RRT	190 (a); 225 (d)
New York	Buffalo	Integrated Waste Systems (IWS)	60 (a); 300 (d)
New York	Islip	Town of Islip	125 (a); 300 (d)
New York	Syracuse	RRT-Empire Returns	300 (a); 300 (d)
No. Carolina	Charlotte	Fairfield Co. Recy.	100 (a); 130 (d)
Ohio	Beaver Creek	Koogler-Suburban/WMI	30 (a); 50 (d)
Pennsylvania	Erie	WMI	40 (a); 333 (d)
Pennsylvania	Philadelphia	Waste Mgmt-The Forge	200 (d)
Pennsylvania	Pittsburgh	Chambers Development/ American Recycling	60 (a)
Rhode Island	Johnston	Rhode Island SWMC	200 (a); 140 (d)
So. Carolina	Charleston	Charleston County	100 (d)
Tennessee	Kingsport	WMI	40 (a); 60 (d)
Texas	Austin	ACCO Waste Paper	40 (a); 120 (d)
Virginia	Roanoke	Cycle Systems	1 (a)
Washington	Seattle	Rabanco	300 (a); 400 (d)
Wisconsin	Milwaukee	Peltz Bros./WMI	30 (a); 40 (d)

Source: Glenn, "MRF's in the U.S.," *Biocycle,* July 1991, pp. 31–32, 34, 36–37.
a = actual; d = design

Appendix 3.2A

VENDORS OF COMPLETE MRF FACILITIES OR OPERATING SERVICES

Alcoa Recyling Machinery Service, 2665 Riverport Rd., Memphis, Tenn. 38109

Attwoods, Inc., 2601 So. Bayshire Dr., Coconut Grove, Fla. 33133

Browning Ferris Industries, P.O. Box 3151, Houston, Tex. 77253

Chambers Development, 10700 Frankstown Rd., Pittsburgh, Pa. 15235

CRInc., 74 Salem Rd., North Billerica, Mass. 01862

Daneco, 450 Park Ave., Suite 2104, New York, N.Y. 10022

Dominion Recycling Systems, P.O. Box 1065, Charlottesville, Va. 22902

Fairfield Co. Recycling, 1300 Honeyspot Rd. Ext., Stratford, Conn. 06497

Materials Recycling Corp., 20600 Chagrin Blvd., Cleveland, Ohio 44122

National Ecology Co., 16 Greenmeadow Dr., Timonium, Md. 21093

Omni Technical Service, 50 Charles Lindbergh Blvd., Uniondale, N.Y. 11553

Recycle Systems, 1533 120th Ave. N.E., P.O. Box 1691, Bellingham, Wash. 98009

Resource Recovery Systems, 36 Plains Rd., Essex, Conn. 06426

RRT-Empire Returns, P.O. Box 536, Syracuse, N.Y. 13211–0536

Waste Management, Inc., 3003 Butterfield Rd., Oakbrook, Ill. 60521

Western Waste Industries, 11125 W. 190th St., Gardena, Calif. 90248

Source: Glenn, "MRF's in the U.S.," *Biocycle*, July 1991, p. 77.

Appendix 3.2B

VENDORS OF MRF EQUIPMENT ONLY

AR Products, P.O. Box 1638, Monroe, N.C. 28111

Bruce Mooney Associates, 1849 Fairhill Rd., Allison Park, Pa. 15101

Count Recycling Systems, 443 SW 6th St., Des Moines, Iowa 50309

CP Manufacturing, Inc., 1428 McKinley Ave., National City, Calif. 92050

Dover Conveyor, P.O. Box 300, Midvale, Ohio 44653

Duraquip, Inc., P.O. Box 948, Tualatin, Oreg. 97062

The Heil Co., 205 Bishops Way, Suite 201, Brooksfield, Wis. 53005

Hustler Conveyor Co., 4985 Fyler Ave., St. Louis, Mo. 63139

Jorgensen Conveyors, Inc., 10303 N. Baehr Rd., Mequon, Wis. 53092–4611

Karl Schmidt & Associates, Inc., 44 S. Fox St., Denver, Colo. 80223

Kloosterman Environmental Equip., P.O. Box 85, Alliston, Ontario, Canada LOM 1A0

Lindemann Recycling Equipment, 42 W. 38th St., 11th Fl., New York, N.Y. 10018

Lummus Development, P.O. Box 2526, Columbus, Ga. 31902

Magnificent Machinery, 2366 Woodhill Rd., Cleveland, Ohio 44106

Mayfran International, P.O. Box 43038, Cleveland, Ohio 44143

Miller Manufacturing, P.O. Box 336, Turlock, Calif. 95381

Mosley Machinery Co., Inc., P.O. Box 1552, Waco, Tex. 76703–1552

New London Engineering, 1700 Division St., New London, Wis. 54961

Prab Conveyors, P.O. Box 2121, Kalamazoo, Mich. 49003

Ptarmigan Machinery Co., 217 San Anselmo, Suite B, San Anselmo, Calif. 94960

Recycling Equipment Mfg., Inc., S. 2207 Lawson, Airway Hgts., Wash. 99001

Resource Technology, Inc., P.O. Box 251, Van Meter, Iowa 50261

Rexnord, P.O. Box 2022, Milwaukee, Wis. 53201
Serpentix Conveyor Corp., 9085 Marshall Court, Westminster, Colo. 80030
Van Dyk Baler Corp., 1033 Route 46, Clifton, N.J. 07013

Source: Glenn, "MRF's in the U.S.," *Biocycle*, July 1991, pp. 75–77.

Appendix 3.3

VENDORS OF CURBSIDE RECYCLING COLLECTION
TRUCKS/TRAILERS

Able Body Co., Inc., P.O. Box 891, Newark, Calif. 94560

Eager Beaver Mfg., General Engines, Interstate 295, Thorofare, N.J. 08086

Hiab Cranes & Loaders, 34 Blevins, Suite 10, New Castle, Del. 19720

Hydron, Inc./Recycling Div., 237 Weymouth St., Rockland, Mass. 02370

J.V. Manufacturing, Inc., P.O. Box 229, Springdale, Ariz. 72765

Kann Manufacturing Corp., 414 N. Third St., Guttenberg, Iowa 52052

Labrie Equipment Ltd., 302, rue du Fleuve, Beaumont, PQ GOR 1CO0, Canada

Lodal, Inc., P.O. Box 2315, Kingsford, Mich. 49801

Marrel Corp., 131 Indian Lake Rd., Hendersonville, Tenn. 37075

Multitek, Inc., 700 Main St., Prentice, Wis. 54556

Waste Control Systems, Inc., 220 Lawton St., Ludlow, Mass. 01056

Source: New Hampshire Resource Recovery Association, *Recycling in New Hampshire*, 1988, pp. 110–111.

Appendix 3.4

SELECTED LOCATIONS USING MIXED WASTE PROCESSING

LOCATION	TYPE OF WASTE	THROUGHPUT (TONS/DAY)	START-UP DATE
Buena Vista, IA	Resid./Comm.	Rated at 100	Dec., 1990
High Point, NC	Resid./Comm.	Rated at 550	Feb., 1991
Newport Beach, CA	Resid.	Rated at 150	Jan., 1991
Bremen, OH	(Under Development)		
Etobicoke, Ont.	Comm./Ind.	Rated at 600	1990
Nanaimo, B.C.	(Under Development)		

Source: Steve Apotheker, "Mixed Waste Processing," *Resource Recycling* 10, September 1991, p. 33

Appendix 3.5A

VENDORS OF PLASTIC GRANULATORS

Alpine American Corp., 5 Michigan Dr., Natick, Mass. 01760

American Pulverizer Co., 5540 West Park Ave., St. Louis, Mo. 63110

Ball & Jewell Div., Sterling, Inc., 5200 W. Clinton, Milwaukee, Wis. 53223

Berner Industries, P.O. Box 8228, New Castle, Pa. 16107

Berstorff Corp., P.O. Box 240357, Charlotte, N.C. 28224

Buss-Condux, 2411 United Lane, Elk Grove Village, Ill. 60007

Complete Systems Co., Inc., P.O. Box 1276, Londonderry, N.H. 03053

Foremost Machine Builders, P.O. Box 644, 23 Spielman, Fairfield, N.J. 07006

Herbold Granulators USA, Inc., 36 Maple Ave., Seekonk, Mass. 02771

Nelmor Co., Inc., An AEC Company, Rivulet St., N. Uxbridge, Mass. 01538

Pallmann Pulverizers Co., Inc., 820 Bloomfield Ave., Clifton, N.J. 07012

Source: New Hampshire Resource Recovery Association, *Recycling in New Hampshire*, 1988, p. 112.

Appendix 3.5B

VENDORS OF GLASS CRUSHERS

American Pulverizer Co., Inc., 5540 W. Park Ave., St. Louis, Mo. 63110

Baler Equipment Co., P.O. Drawer 1837, Portland, Oreg. 97207

Count Co., P.O. Box 3119, Des Moines, Iowa 50316

CP Manufacturing, Inc., 1428 McKinley Ave., National City, Calif. 92050

C.S. Bell Co., P.O. Box 291, Tiffin, Ohio 44883

Dens-A-Can International, 1849 Fairhill Rd., Allison Park, Pa. 15101

Dresser Industries, Jeffrey Division, P.O. Box 387, Woodruff, S.C. 29388

Ertel Engineering Co., P.O. Box 3245, Kingston, N.Y. 12401

Galland Henning Nopak, Inc., P.O. Box 15500, Milwaukee, Wis. 53215

The G.E.W. Co., Inc., P.O. Box 376, Branford, Conn. 06405

Grassan Equipment Co., P.O. Box 714, Mansfield, Ohio 44903

Gruendler Crusher, 212 S. Oak Street, Durand, Mich. 48429

Hi-Torque Shredder Co., 230 Sherman Ave., Berkeley Heights, N.J. 07922

Jacobson, Inc., 2445 Nevada Avenue North, Minneapolis, Minn. 55427

Miller Manufacturing Co., P.O. Box 336, Turlock, Calif. 95381

Orwak USA, Inc., 10816 Normandale Blvd., Minneapolis, Minn. 55437

Prodeva, Inc., Drawer R, Jackson Center, Ohio 45334

Recycling Equipment Mfg., N. 6512 Napa, Spokane, Wash. 99207

Shredding Systems, Inc., P.O. Box 869, Wilsonville, Oreg. 97070

Source: NHRRA, 1988, p. 111.

Appendix 3.5C

VENDORS OF PAPER SHREDDERS

American Pulverizer Co., 5540 W. Park Ave., St. Louis, Mo. 63110

Balemaster, 980 Crown Court, Crown Point, Ind. 46307

Baler Equipment Co., P.O. Drawer 1837, Portland, Oreg. 97207

Balewel, Box 465, Crown Point, Ind. 46307

Ball & Jewell Div., Sterling, Inc., 5200 W. Clinton, Milwaukee, Wis. 53223

Carthage Machine Co., 571 West End Ave., Carthage, N.Y. 13619

Counselor Engineering, Inc., P.O. Box 428, Hudson, Ohio 44236

D & J Wendt Corp., P.O. Box 888, North Tonawanda, N.Y. 14120

Dresser Industries, Jeffrey Division, P.O. Box 387, Woodruff, S.C. 29388

East Chicago Machine Tool, P.O. Box 465, Crown Point, Ind. 46307

Gruendler Crusher, 212 S. Oak St., Durand, Mich. 48429

Hi-Torque Shredder Co., 230 Sherman Ave., Berkeley Heights, N.J. 07922

Industrial Paper Shredders, Inc., P.O. Box 180, Salem, Ohio 44460

Jacobson, Inc., 2445 Nevada Ave. North, Minneapolis, Minn. 55427

Lindemann Recycling Equipment, Inc., 500 Fifth Ave., New York, N.Y. 10110

Montgomery Industries International, Inc., P.O. Box 3687, Jacksonville, Fla. 32206

Resource Technology Corp., P.O. Box 506, 200 Milton, Dedham, Mass. 02061

Shred Pax Corp., 136 W. Commercial Ave., Wood Dale, Ill. 60191-1304

Shredding Systems, Inc., P.O. Box 869, Wilsonville, Oreg. 97070

Universal Engineering Corp., 800 1st Ave. N.W., Cedar Rapids, Iowa 52405

Van Dyk Baler Corp., 234 Fifth Ave., New York, N.Y. 10001

Source: NHRRA, 1988, p. 108.

Appendix 3.5D

VARIOUS TYPES OF INDUSTRIAL BALERS

Baler Type	General Description	Advantages/Disadvantages	Cost
Horizontal	High-speed, high-capacity machine, primarily used in very large programs. Can produce multiple bales in one hour.	Able to process large quantity of materials in a short time. Minimal labor needed to produce bales. Bales are easy to unload. Requires adequate storage area.	$18,000 to $30,000, depending on intake.
Vertical			
Upstroke	Bales are produced by compression from below. Also called "pit" baler, because material is loaded into a pit below surface level.	Able to process bales quickly. Material loaded directly from floor surface, and pushed into baler by force of gravity. Relatively low-labor	$15,000 to $20,000, plus special "pit" construction

Baler Type	General Description	Advantages/Disadvantages	Cost
Vertical			
Upstroke	Can produce multiple bales per hour.	intensive, bales produced rather quickly. Bales are easy to unload, as they are at surface level. Requires construction of a pit in floor below baler to install.	
Downstroke	Bales are produced compression from above. Commonly used in small recycling programs. Generally produces one bale per hour, depending on operator.	Least expensive type of baler. Storage needs are minimal, and baler can be easily installed on any flat concrete, steel, or heavy-duty wood surface. High labor needs. Bales take longer to produce, since material must be lifted up manually from the floor and put into baler.	$6,000 to $12,000

Source: NHRRA, 1988, p. 28.

Appendix 3.5E

VENDORS OF BALERS

American Baler Co., P.O. Box 919, Brunswick, Maine 04011

Ameri-Shred Corp., P.O. Box 46130, Monroeville, Pa. 15146

Balemaster, 980 Crown Point Court, Crown Point, Ind. 46307

Baler Equipment Co., P.O. Box 496, Belgrade Lakes, Maine 04918

C and M Co., 52 Center St., Portland, Maine 04101

Cive Recycling, Inc., Route 12 South, Marlborough, N.H. 03455

East Chicago Machine, P.O. Box 465, Crown Point, Ind. 46307

Econ Scrap Shear Co., 540 Cordele Rd., Albany, Ga. 31705

Enterprise Baler Co., 616 South Santa Fe St., Santa Ana, Calif. 92705

Fox Manufacturing Co., 345 Nutmeg Rd. South, S. Windsor, Conn. 06074

Global Equipment, Inc., East 10310 Montgomery, Spokane, Wash. 99206

Harmony Enterprises, 706 Main Ave. North, Harmony, Minn. 55939

The Harris Group, 1700 Landmark Tower, 345 St. Peter St., St. Paul, Minn. 55102

International Baler Corp., P.O. Box 6922, Jacksonville, Fla. 32236

J.V. Manufacturing, P.O. Box 229, Springdale, Ariz. 72765

Kilkom, Inc., Industrial Park Building 6, Spokane, Wash. 99216

K-Metal Fabrication, 300 Linton Ave., Croydon, Pa. 19020

Lindemann Recycling Equipment, Inc., 500 Fifth Ave., New York, N.Y. 10110

Load King Manufacturing Co., P.O. Box 50398, New Bedford, Mass. 02745

Logemann Brother Co., 3150 South Burleigh St., Milwaukee, Wis. 53210

Lummus Development Corp., P.O. Box 2526, Columbus, Ga. 31902

Marathon Equipment Co., P.O. Box 290, Clearfield, Pa. 16830

Maren Engineering Corp., P.O. Box 485A, Concord, N.H. 03302–0485

McDonald Services, Inc., P.O. Box 561238, Charlotte, N.C. 28256

Mosley Machinery Co., 1411 Patrick Court, Maple Glen, Pa. 19002

Northwest Design and Equipment Co., Inc., N. 2020 Dollar Road, Spokane, Wash. 99212

Philadelphia Tramrail Co., 2207 East Ontario St., Philadelphia, Pa. 19134

Seyco Textile Machinery, P.O. Box 7580, Chicago, Ill. 60680

Source Recycling Systems, 9949 West 25th Ave., Lakewood, Colo. 80215

Van Dyk Baler Corp., 1033 Route 46, Clifton, N.J. 07013

Waco Products, Inc., P.O. Box 829, Troy, Ohio 45373

Waste Processing Equipment, P.O. Box 1047, Rainsville, Ala. 35986

Waste Technology, Inc., 738 East Burnside, Suite 3, Portland, Oreg. 97214

Source: New Hampshire Governor's Recycling Program, "N.H. Recycling Equipment Bulletin E1," January 1991.

Appendix 3.5F

VENDORS OF BALING SUPPLIES

American Baler Co., Economy Baler Div., 200 Hickory, Bellevue, Ohio 44811

Atlantic Shippers Supply Co., Pine Street Extension, Nashua, N.H. 03060

Baler Equipment Co., P.O. Drawer 1837, Portland, Oreg. 97207

The Beehive, P.O. Box 487, Hammond, Ind. 46320

Caristrap International, Inc., 1760 Boulevard Fortin, Laval, PQ H7S 1N8, Canada

Cavert Wire Co., P.O. Box 1167, Uniontown, Pa. 15401

Coastal Wire Co., Inc., Rt. 2, Box 205-M, Andrews, S.C. 29510

Cranston Machinery Co., Inc., P.O. Box 68207, Oak Grove, Oreg. 97268

Harry Stoller & Son, 113 Essex St., Haverhill, Mass. 01830

International Baler Corp., P.O. Box 6922, Jacksonville, Fla. 32236

Parade Wire Products, P.O. Box 360, Bensalem, Pa. 19020

Recycle Systems, P.O. Box 1691, Bellevue, Wash. 98008

Reftech, Inc., 361 Delaware St., Suite 311, Buffalo, N.Y. 14202

Selco Products, Inc., P.O. Box 406, Baxley, Ga. 31513

TFC Corp., 9819 Logan Avenue S., Minneapolis, Minn. 55431

USS Packaging System, 13535 S. Torrence Ave., Chicago, Ill. 60633

Source: New Hampshire Resource Recovery Association, *Recycling in New Hampshire,* 1988, pp. 108–109.

Appendix 3.5G

VENDORS OF WOOD SHREDDERS

American Pulverizer Co., 5540 W. Park Ave., St. Louis, Mo. 63110

Continental Biomass Ind., 66 Pelham Rd., Salem, N.H. 03079

Counselor Engineering Inc., P.O. Box 428, Hudson, Ohio 44236

Dresser Industries, Jeffrey Div., P.O. Box 387, Woodruff, S.C. 29388

Environmental Resource Return Co., P.O. Box 3096, Portsmouth, N.H. 03801

Fuel Harvesters Equip. Inc., 12759 Loma Rica Dr., Grass Valley, Calif. 95945

Gruendler Crusher, 212 S. Oak St., Durand, Mich. 48429

Hi-Torque Shredder Co., 230 Sherman Ave., Berkeley Heights, N.J. 07922

Jacobson, Inc., 2445 Nevada Ave. N., Minneapolis, Minn. 55427

LaBounty Manufacturing, Inc., State Road 2, P.O. Box B, Two Harbors, Minn. 55616

Lindemann Recycling Equip. Inc., 500 Fifth Ave., New York, N.Y. 10110

Lindig Manufacturing Corp., 1875 W. County Road C, St. Paul, Minn. 55113

Montgomery Industries International, Inc., P.O. Box 3687, Jacksonville, Fla. 32206

Morbark Industries, Inc., P.O. Box 1000, Winn, Mich. 48896

Pallman Pulverizers Co., Inc., 820 Bloomfield Ave., Clifton, N.J. 07012

Shredding Systems, Inc., P.O. Box 869, Wilsonville, Oreg. 97070

Shred Pax Corp., 136 W. Commercial Ave., Wood Dale, Ill. 60191-1304

Universal Engineering Corp., 800 1st Avenue, Cedar Rapids, Iowa 52405

Universal Refiner Distributors Corp., P.O. Box 125, Parlin, N.J. 08859

Source: NHRRA, 1988, p. 114A.

Appendix 3.6

A GUIDE FOR SORTING SCRAP METAL

(Refer to Table 2.5 for lists of metal products easy to identify. Appendix 3.6 is for any materials not on lists of common products.)

1. Is it light iron? That is — is the metal thin (less than ¼-inch thick) sheet iron or light-weight ferrous tubing which can be compacted and shredded? A magnet is the tool needed to identify and sort aluminum and other nonferrous metals from ferrous.

2. Is it primarily metal, such as an appliance?

3. If the answer is yes to these two questions, then it goes in pile 1, 2, or 3.

   • Pile 1 is free of hazardous contaminants or the possible danger of explosion.

   • Pile 2 is all appliances.

   • Pile 3 is contaminated iron, such as exhaust systems, or dangerous containers that had oil, solvent or other chemical residues.

All other items are not light iron and should be sorted into separate groups:

1. *Wire:* Wire or cable (incl. fencing) should be cut into lengths 3 feet or less and stored separately. This prevents it from tangling with other materials in the press which slows down production.

2. *Other Metals:* Aluminum, cast iron, heavy steel (¼-inch thick), brass, and copper are of value and should be stored in separate piles to be sold.

3. *Non-Metals:* All rubber, wood, and some plastics and fabric must be removed from your scrap metal.

Look for and separate these materials: Some of the items will require the use of your magnet.

Item	Common Contaminants
White Goods	Fiberglass water tanks, plastic box fans, appliances stuffed with other junk. Do not fill refrigerators with small appliances.
Sheet Metal	Aluminum siding and gutters, wood frames attached to sheet metal.
Furniture	Aluminum mail boxes, chairs or clothes drying racks. Plastic or wood chair seats and table tops. Metal legs are OK. Bedframes/headboards without springs, strapping, etc. Also make sure barbecue grills are not cast aluminum.
Toys & Recreation	Bicycle tires, concrete attached to swing set poles, engines and gas tanks.
Car Parts	Tires, engine blocks, cast axles, gas tanks, exhaust parts, fiberglass body parts. Some truck caps are aluminum or have wood framework.
Tools	Wood and plastic handles, aluminum snow shovels, engine and gas tanks.

Please make sure all gas tanks or cans, etc. are completely empty before placing in your pile 3 (#2 light iron).

Source: NHRRA, 1988, p. 97.

Appendix 4.1

THE GAIN FROM MANAGING SCRAP METAL

New Hampshire Resource Recovery Association
COOPERATIVE SCRAP METAL MARKETING PROGRAM
Example of charges and revenues
Revised 7/21/88

NOTE: The figures below are APPROXIMATE examples if your pile has 100 tons of scrap metal and is located 50 miles from the nearest market.

CHARGES TO PROCESS SCRAP METAL

	UNMANAGED PILE	SEPARATED PILES*
1. Transfer of Baling Press		
$3/mile to move from previous site	$ 90	$ 90
to your site (average = 30 miles)		
2. Baling Press Rental Charge		
$75/hour for each hour operating	$5325	$2700
Separated piles average 2.8 tons/hour	(71 hours)	(36 hours)
Unmanaged piles average 1.4 tons/hour		
3. Loading Charge		
$50/load X number of loads	$ 250	$ 250
required to move metal to market.		
(100 tons = 5 loads)		

	UNMANAGED PILE	SEPARATED PILES*

4. Freight Miles

$3/loaded mile X number of loads required to move metal to market.

(100 tons = 5 loads)

	UNMANAGED PILE	SEPARATED PILES*
4. Freight Miles	$ 750	$ 750

5. NHRRA Fee

	UNMANAGED PILE	SEPARATED PILES*
$1/ton members, $3/ton non-members	$ 100	$ 100
Total Charges for Processing	$6515	$3890

REVENUES FROM SALE OF SCRAP METAL

		UNMANAGED PILE		SEPARATED PILES*
6. Revenue from Sale of Metals				
#1 Light Iron at $25/ton*	(45 tons)	$1125	(60 tons)	$1500
#2 Light Iron at $20/ton*	(55 tons)	$1100	(35 tons)	$ 700
Aluminum, cast iron & heavy steel scrap at $400/ton Avg*	(0 tons)	$ 0	(5 tons)	$2000
Total Revenue from Sales		$2225		$4200
7. Net Cost to Municipality		$6515	Expense	$3890
		− 2225	Revenue	− 4200
	Net Cost	$4290	Net Revenue	$ 310

Source: NHRRA, 1988, p. 99.

Note: NHRRA's experience since June 1, 1986 indicates that separating scrap into five piles, #1 light iron, #2 light iron, aluminum, cast iron, and heavy steel increases the percentage of #1 light iron scrap and decreases costly baling time.

*Separated into the three categories under 6.

Appendix 5.1

SOLID WASTE ORDINANCE

TOWN OF CHESTERFIELD, N.H.
Office of Selectmen

SOLID WASTE ORDINANCE

Effective Date: July 1, 1989
*Hearing — amended 08/03/89
**Hearing — amended 11/09/89
***Hearing — amended 03/15/90
****Hearing — amended 08/22/91

Pursuant to the authority of RSA 31:39 and the authority granted by Town Meeting 1988 and affirmed at Town Meeting 1989 the Selectmen of the Town of Chesterfield hereby adopt the following ordinance for the operation of a public transfer station and recycling facility.

1. ADMISSION:
   The Transfer Station — Recycling Facility will be open for use by Town residents and non-resident property owners. Admission to the Facility will be only by permit issued annually, available at the Selectmen's Office. All permits must be attached to a motor vehicle or plainly visible.
   Persons who own property in the Town for rent must apply to the Selectmen's Office for permits for their tenants to use the Facility. One permit will be issued for each dwelling unit. The permit will be furnished to the owner upon payment of an administrative fee of $5.00 per permit on a laminated card which shall be transferable to subsequent renters.
   Hours for the Facility shall be as follows:

** Mon. & Tues.   8:00 A.M.–10:00 A.M.   1:00 P.M.–5:00 P.M.
   Fri.   8:00 P.M.–10:00 P.M.   12:00–5:00 P.M.
   Sat.   8:00 A.M.–5:00 P.M.

No brush will be accepted on Tues. due to burning.
* Refuse generated within the Town of Chesterfield and transported by commercial haulers will be accepted provided the recyclables are separated as required and the containers for the compactors are marked with the originator's name. Commercial haulers shall be those who haul refuse to the Facility for a fee, excluding mechanical compactors.

2. SEPARATION

All material brought to the Facility for disposal shall be separated into the following categories to be deposited in designated containers or locations as the Attendant directs.

SEPARATED GOODS

A. GLASS:

Clean, rinsed and empty GREEN, BLUE, BROWN or CLEAR glass with all plastic metal pieces removed.

NOT ALLOWED
window glass, light bulbs and ceramics

B. PLASTIC:

Clear and colored plastic containers ****removed (soda, milk, cider, juice, etc.)

C. PAPER:

Separated by newspaper, corrugated paper, brown paper bags, and magazines. ****add mixed paper

D. ALUMINUM CANS:

Refundable and Non-refundable

E. LARGE METAL OBJECTS:

All scrap metal (i.e. bedsprings) except as excluded

F. WHITE METAL:

Household appliances ($ fee charged)

G. TIRES:

All tires, removed from wheel or rim ($ fee charged)

H. LEAVES & CLIPPINGS:

Lawn clippings, green and dry waste, compostables placed in compost pile. Non-biodegradable containers (i.e. plastic bags) must be removed to compactor.

I. TREE LIMBS/BRUSH:

Material 5" and less at butt end

J. BUILDING MATERIALS:

Separated burnable/non-burnable. Contractors with special permit from Selectmen's Office—Residents with Building permit.

K. MOTOR OIL:

In capped, leakproof container

L. AUTOMOBILE BATTERIES: Other batteries to be deposited in receptical at the Facility.

M. HOUSEHOLD TRASH/GARBAGE: Shall mean any other residential waste not otherwise listed and shall be placed in compactor.

N. BULKY ITEMS: Couches, mattresses, televisions, etc.

O. ****TIN/STEEL CANS (added)

NOTE: ALL ITEMS NOT NOTED AS RECYCLABLE OR EXCLUDED WILL GO INTO THE COMPACTOR—See M. above.

3. UNACCEPTABLE MATERIALS:
    The following goods ARE NOT ALLOWED at the Facility

A. DEAD ANIMALS

B. STUMPS/TREES/LAND CLEARING WASTE

C. HAZARDOUS WASTE: (Hold for Hazardous Waste Collection Day—
                to be posted)

Septic sludge or septic waste	Gasoline
Bug sprays	Kerosene
Floor Care Products	Motor Oil
Furniture Products	Other Oils
Metal Polish w/solvent	Paint Brush cleaner w/solvent
Automatic Transmission Fluid	Glue (solvent based)
Battery Acid	Paint—oil based
Brake Fluid	Paint—auto
Car Wax Solvent	Paint—model
Diesel Fuel	Paint thinner
Fuel Oil	Paint stripper
Fungicide	Primer
Herbicide	Turpentine
Insecticide	Varnish
Rat poison	Wood preservative
Weed Killer	
Ammunition	Mercury batteries
Artists Paints, mediums	Moth Balls
Dry Cleaning solvents	Old Fire Arms
Fiberglass epoxy	Photographic chemicals
Gun cleaning solvents	(unmixed)
Lighter fluid	Swimming Pool acid
Explosives	Hospital or vet waste
Toxic Waste	Pressure Treated woods
Gas tanks	Catalitic converters

D. AUTOMOBILES, BOATS, MOTORCYCLES, SNOWMOBILES
will NOT BE ACCEPTED
(EXCEPTION – EXHAUST SYSTEMS) *(remove-fee of $1.00 per system)
ANY ITEMS WHICH, IN THE OPINION OF THE ATTENDANT CONSTITUTE
A HAZARD TO EMPLOYEES, TO OTHER USERS OF THE FACILITY, OR TO
THE PROPERTY OF THE TOWN.
ANY MATERIAL LISTED AS UNACCEPTABLE IN THE NH REAs OR THE
DEPARTMENT OF ENVIRONMENTAL SERVICES ADMINISTRATIVE RULES
OR PROHIBITED ON THE TOWN'S PERMIT TO OPERATE THE FACILITY.

4. SUPERVISION

1. The transfer station Attendants and the Board of Selectmen shall have the sole authority to grant or deny access to the Facility.

2. The Attendants shall have full authority to direct the use of the Facility by the public. Failure to follow the directions of the attendants shall be a violation of this ordinance.

3. Disposal fees shall be collected for those items accepted at the Facility for which the Town must pay an additional fee for removal by private contractor according to the following schedule:

(Payment shall be made to the attendant before the item is accepted for disposal)

****APPLIANCES	$5.00 each
****TIRES	$1.00
****add – TRUCK TIRES	$2.00
****add – LOADER TIRES	$5.00

4. A part of this ordinance shall be the continuation of the Recycling Committee established as an ad hoc committee serving at the pleasure of the Selectmen at Town Meeting 1988. It shall be the goal of this committee to advise the Selectmen on the operation of the facility, to offer advice on the refinement of the recycling effort and to assist the town in finding and maintaining markets for recyclable goods.

5. All revenues received from the operation of the Facility shall be used solely to offset the cost of refuse disposal for the Town.

5. VIOLATIONS:
It shall be a violation of this ordinance and other Town and State ordinances to dump trash at or near the gate to the Facility, to dispose of trash along the roadways or to maintain "home dumps" to avoid the intent of this Ordinance to recycle. The gate will be locked at all times when the Facility is not open to the public. Anyone entering the Facility when the gate is locked is guilty of trespass and shall be charged with violating the terms of this Ordinance.
It shall be a violation of this Ordinance to DISCHARGE A FIREARM at the Facility.
BURNING at the Facility shall be carried out only with the approval of the District Fire Warden and within the limits of the Town's permit to operate the Facility.

ONLY MATERIALS GENERATED WITHIN THE LIMITS OF THE TOWN OF CHESTERFIELD SHALL BE ACCEPTED AT THE FACILITY.

Authorized users of the Facility must contact the Town Offices for a dated permit to allow contractors to dispose of acceptable materials generated at their residence or place of business in Chesterfield.

It shall be a violation of this Ordinance to attempt to dispose of prohibited items or to dispose of items in a manner that does not comply with this Ordinance.

Containers shall be opened at the request of the attendant to verify that recyclable goods are being separated and disposed of properly. Failure to comply with this request shall be a violation of this Ordinance.

6. PENALTY:

Any person or corporation guilty of violating any provision of this Ordinance shall be fined $100 for each such violation, payable to the Selectmen's Office within five (5) working days.

7. PROVISIONS:

This Ordinance shall not be amended except by the Selectmen after a public hearing. The validity of any provision of this Ordinance shall not affect the validity of any other provision nor the validity of the Ordinance as a whole.

Given under our hand and seal this date:
June 8, 1989
Stephen L. Laskowski
Harold C. Nowill
Elizabeth A. Benjamin
Chesterfield Selectmen

Public Hearing Date: June 1, 1989
" Amended 8/3/89
" Amended 11/9/89
" Amended 3/15/90

Elizabeth A. Benjamin, Chrm.
James E. Machleid
Harold C. Nowill
Chesterfield Selectmen
8/22/91

" Amended 8/22/91

Source: Chesterfield, N.H., 1991.

Appendix 5.2

RECYCLING AWARENESS IN SCHOOL: AN EXAMPLE

The importance of recycling can be integrated in classroom instruction in subjects as diverse as arithmetic, economics, social and political science, and environmental awareness. The following is an example of using recycling to teach second graders a little arithmetic, using money, the kinds of jobs people have, a little about how their town works, and of course trash disposal and recycling.

Materials Needed

A large sack containing both recyclables and (clean) trash, a large cardboard box, play money, markers, and plain paper.

(The example below uses a character named Recycleman.)

Steps

1. Children select roles to play. We need someone to run the dump, landfill, or incinerator. (They get the large cardboard box and write *dump, landfill,* or *incinerator* on it.) We need both a town trash hauler and a collector of recyclables, buyers for various separated materials, and an appropriate town official or two. The children make signs indicating who they are.

2. Distribute money to the children, the buyers getting fairly small amounts and the town officials getting the rest.

3. Recycleman dumps the bag out and shows the children all the solid waste. He then returns it to the bag and turns it over to the town officials.

4. Town officials give the bag to their trash hauler and also give the hauler a sum of money. Write the amount on the board—say, $50 per bag.

5. The hauler brings the bag to the dump and pays the attendant the money. The attendant puts the bag in the large box.

6. Now have the town officials decide to recycle. Recycleman retrieves the bag and dumps the trash out again. The collector of recyclables pulls out all the materials that can be sold; the remainder goes back in the bag. The now smaller bag is given back to the town officials.

7. Town officials call for each various buyer to come up, and the buyers give town officials money for the appropriate material. The collector gives the money to the town officials; the figure is written on the board separate from the $50.

8. Town officials still have to get rid of the bag and make a big deal about how it is smaller than before and should therefore only cost $25 to get rid of. They give the $25 to the trash hauler, who gives it and the bag to the dump attendant.

9. Now the class must figure out how much it costs to get rid of the bag in each situation. [Answer: $50 in the first case, and $25 minus the sale revenues in the second.]

10. This shows both kinds of gains from recycling, "costs avoided" and sale revenue.

Many variations on this example are possible.

Appendix 5.3

EDUCATIONAL MATERIALS ON RECYCLING

A-Way with Waste: A Waste Management Curriculum for Schools. 2nd edition, Washington State Department of Ecology, 4350 150th Ave. N.E., Redmond, Wash. 98052. Contact: Jan Lingenfelter.

Biogradable, A Science Unit for 4th Grade. Columbus Clean Community, 181 So. Washington Blvd., Columbus, Ohio 43215

A Case of Waste. 4-H Youth and Development Office, Box 4, Robert Hall, Cornell University, Ithaca, N.Y. 14850. Contact: MaryLou Brewer.

Don't Waste Waste! Environmental Action Coalition, 625 Broadway, New York, N.Y. 10012. (212) 677-1601.

Eco-News. Environmental Action Coalition, 625 Broadway, New York, N.Y. 10012. (212) 677-1601. Ask for back issues related to recycling.

The Great Glass Caper: An Educational Kit. Pennsylvania Glass Recycling Corp., 509 N. Second St., Harrisburg, Pa. 17101. (717) 234-8091. Materials are geared toward 4th, 5th and 6th grades. Contact: Doug Gibboney.

Here Today, Here Tomorrow: A Curriculum on Recycling, Energy, Solid Waste. Conservation and Environmental Studies Center, Inc., 120-13 Whitesbog Rd., Browns Mills, N.J. 08015. Developed in conjunction with the New Jersey Department of Energy, Office of Recycling.

Let's Recycle! Instructional Worksheets and Activities. Office of Recycling, Department of Waste Management, Town of Brookhaven, 3233 Route 112, Medford, N.Y. 11763. (516) 451-6220. Contact: Elaine Maas. Available to Town of Brookhaven teachers who have taken part in the Recycling Education Program.

Let's Recycle! Lesson Plans for Grades K–6 and 7–12. U.S. Environmental Protection Agency. (SW-801), 1980. Office of Water and Waste Management, Washington, D.C. 20460.

The Lone Recycler: A Comic Book on Recycling. Materials World Publishing, 1089 Curtis, Albany, Calif. 94706.

Oscar's Options. Department of Environmental Management, State of Rhode Island, 9 Hayes St., Providence, R.I. 02908. (401) 277-3434. Contact: Carole Bell, curriculum guide.

Out of Sight, Out of Mind? A Guide to Solid Waste and Recycling Investigations for Kindergarten through Sixth Grade. Sage Recycling, P.O. Box 1001, Boulder, Colo. 80306.

Publicity and Education for Recycling: An Informative Guide. Tanis Rickmers-Skislak, 3319 Willow Crescent Dr. #32, Fairfax, Va. 22030.

Recycling for Reuse. Publication 4-H 362, 4-H Program, University of Wisconsin Extension, 328 Lowell Hall, 610 Langdon St., Madison, Wis. 53703. [A curriculum guide will be published in Spring 1988 by the Bureau of Solid Waste, Wisconsin Department of Natural Resources, P.O. Box 7921, Madison, Wis. 53707. (608) 267-7565. Contact: John Reindl.]

Recycling Lesson Plans and Activities, Elementary and Secondary Levels. 108 E. Green St., Ithaca, N.Y. 14850. (607) 673-3470. Contact: Lynn Leopold.

"Recycling Education: Developing a Curriculum." Dan Cotter, *Resource Recycling*, July/August 1985, September/October 1985. P.O. Box 10540, Portland, Oreg. 97210. (503) 227-1319.

Super Saver Investigators. Office of Litter Prevention, Ohio Department of Natural Resources, Fountain Square, Building F, Columbus, Ohio 43224. (614) 265-6444. Contact: David Landis. An elementary interdisciplinary guide to recycling, solid waste management and littering—to be published early Summer 1988.

Space Station: EARTH. A Recycling Video Program for 4th-5th Grades. Solid Waste Management Division, Snohomish County Public Works, 4th Floor, County Administration Building, Everett, Wash. 98201. (206) 259-9425. Contact: David M. Polis.

Spreading the Word: A Publicity Handbook For Recycling. Association of New Jersey Environmental Commissions, 300 Mendham Rd., P.O. Box 157, Mendham, N.J. 07945. Contains photo-ready graphics.

The Trash Monster and the Wizard of Waste. California State Department of Education, Publication Sales, P.O. Box 271, Sacramento, Calif. 95802. (916) 445-4688. Recycling education kits (the former for 2nd-3rd grades, the latter for 4th-5th grades).

Woodsy Waste Wise. Cornell Media Services, Audio Visual Resource Center, Building 8, Research Park, Ithaca, N.Y. 14850. (607) 255-2090. Contact: Carol Doolittle. Slides, tape and script, with activities.

Source: NHRRA, 1988, p. 154.

Appendix 5.4

WASTE OIL HEATERS

Arrow Tools/CleanBurn, Mt. Eustis Rd., Littleton, N.H. 03561

Balcrank Products, One Balcrank Way, Weaverville, N.C. 28787

EnviroSystems, Inc., P.O. Box 13, 200 Old River Rd., Bridgewater, Va. 22812

Heating Alternatives, P.O. Box 2078, Great Neck, N.Y. 11022

Lenan Corp., 615 North Parker Dr., Jamesville, Wis. 53545

Orino Waste Oil Heaters, Inc., 114 Franklin St., Rumford, Maine 04276

Wilfred J. Riley/Black Gold, P.O. Box 1549, Dover, N.H. 03820

Sanel Tool & Equipment, 219 S. Main St., Concord, N.H. 03301

SunFire of New England, 290 Smith St., Providence, R.I. 02908

Waste Oil Eliminators/SunFire, P.O. Box 116, Raymond, N.H. 03077

Source: NHRRA, 1988, p. 114.

Appendix 6.1

LEADING NORTH AMERICAN PLASTICS RECYCLERS

Co.	Current Estimated Capacity (million lb/yr)	Projected Capacity By End of '91	Resins
UpNorth Plastics, Grand Prairie, TX	120	140	HDPE/LDPE
Martin Color-fi, Sumter, Trenton, SC	120	150	PET
Wellman, Johnsonville, SC	110	110 +	PET/HDPE
Plastics Recycling Alliance Philadelphia, PA, Chicago, IL	80	n/a	PET/HDPE
MA Industries Peachtree City, GA	60	72	PET/HDPE/PP
NICON Plastics Long Island City, NY	37	37	PET/HDPE

Co.	Current Estimated Capacity (million lb/yr)	Projected Capacity By End of '91	Resins
Day Products Bridgeport, NJ	35	55	PET
Eaglebrook Plastics Chicago, IL	35 (est.)	n/a	HDPE
wTe Recycling/Star Albany, NY	30	30	PET/HDPE
St. Jude Polymer Frackville, PA	15	20 +	PET
AERT Rogers, AR, Junction, TX	27	55	HDPE/LDPE
National PS Recycling Co./ Corona, CA	26	58	PS
Talco Recycling, Inc. Leominster, MA			
Exide Reading, PA	22	24	PP
Johnson Controls Novi, MI	20	same	PET/HDPE
KW Plastics Troy, AL	20	20 +	PP
Envirothene Chino, CA	18	35	PET/HDPE
Pelo Plastic Berthierville, Quebec	15	20	PET/HDPE/LDPE

Co.	Current Estimated Capacity (million lb/yr)	Projected Capacity By End of '91	Resins
Pepsi/Goodyear Pt. Pleasant, WV	14	n/a	PET
Sonoco Graham York, PA	12	20	HDPE
Dart Container Corp. Ontario, FL, Mich, PA	12	same	PS
Clean Tech Dundee, MI	12	same	HDPE
Orion Pacific Odessa, TX	12	24	PET/HDPE
Midwest Plastics Edgertown, WI	10	12	HDPE
Pure Tech Springfield, MA	10	10	PET
Partek Vancouver, WA	6.5	12	HDPE
Hammer Plastics FL, Iowa Falls, IA	6	n/a	PET/misc.
United Resource Recovery Kenton, OH	5	same	HDPE/PP
Polymer Resource Group, Inc. Rosedale, MD	3	10	PET/HDPE
Landfill Alternatives, Inc. Elburn, IL	3	6	Foam PS
Carlisle Plastics Minneapolis, MN	3	6	LDPE

Co.	Current Estimated Capacity (million lb/yr)	Projected Capacity By End of '91	Resins
Quantum Chemical Corp. Heath, OH	0	40	PET/HDPE
Phillips Plastic Recycling Ptnrshp. n/a	0	20-30	HDPE
Union Carbide/Plastics Co. Piscataway, NJ	0	40	PET/HDPE, H/LD film
Exxon/Du Pont Summerville, SC	0	20	PP
Coca-Cola/Hoechst Celanese n/a	0	n/a	n/a
TOTALS	898.5	1,095**	

Source: Society of the Plastics Industry, *Plastics World*, April 1991, p. 80.

n/a indicates data not available

*not yet operational

**Based on lowest figure for data with a range.

The data for this table was provided by the companies listed. All of these companies convert post-consumer plastic waste into pellets, flakes, or a finished plastic product. In some cases data includes post-industrial scrap where it could not be easily separated.

Appendix 6.2

DESCRIPTION OF PROFESSIONAL WASTE DISPOSAL/RECYCLING CONTRACT FOR A HOSPITAL

The contractor shall complete the following services and duties for the Hospital:

1. *Survey.* A comprehensive survey of all facilities occupied by the Hospital's staff will be conducted to determine which buildings/areas will participate in the Program.

2. *Analysis.* An analysis of generation/flow of solid waste recyclable materials will be conducted by the contractor. This analysis will determine the most efficient and least disruptive method of separating solid waste recyclable materials from other waste and storing it for pickup. All appropriate materials will be analyzed by the contractor to determine market value.

3. *Contracts with Dealers/Haulers.* The contractor shall request bids for the sale and removal of solid waste reyclable materials from paper dealers/haulers. The contractor shall prepare and present to the Hospital a list of at least five (5) bids solicited from dealers and/or haulers that are representative of the most competitive prices available. The contractor and the Hospital shall select the winning bid. At the request of the Hospital, the contractor shall negotiate suitable contracts that reflect the best interests of the Hospital and shall submit such contracts to the Hospital for approval. Contractual agreements with appropriate paper dealers/haulers will be secured based on rates offered for recovered material, willingness to commit to agreements which the Hospital deems are in its best interests, and ability to meet all schedule requirements set by the Hospital for removal of recovered materials.

4. *Equipment.* The contractor shall confer with the Hospital regarding the Contractor's recommendations for any equipment that may be needed for the separation, storage and processing of recyclable materials. The Contractor shall present the Hospital with the name of at least three (3) equipment vendors, including information regarding item cost and quality. The Hospital shall in its sole discretion select an equipment vendor, or may at its option purchase the necessary equipment independently.

5. *Presentation of System Proposal.* The Contractor shall present a System Proposal to the Hospital. The System Proposal shall be based on the results of all surveys conducted and shall be the most efficient system to separate, collect and store for pickup all recovered materials.

6. *Training.* The contractor shall provide brochures, posters and other educational materials prior to implementation of the Program. At the request of the Hospital, the Contractor will: (1) assist the Hospital's Public Relations Department in creating such educational materials on an in-house basis; and (2) assist the Hospital's Public Relations Department in publicizing the Program via press releases to local news media.

Training of all participating staff members at the Hospital will be conducted through multi-media seminars to ensure that Hospital employees and other participants understand the operation of the Program. The Contractor will work with the Hospital's Personnel/Training and Development staff to tailor the seminars to maximize the benefit of the seminars to the Hospital's employees.

Source: Emerson Hospital, Concord, Mass., 1992.

Appendix 6.3

RECYCLING OFFICE WASTE PAPER

Why Should Businesses Recycle Their Office Paper?

Office building waste streams are composed primarily of various grades of paper. Every year, most businesses dispose of many tons of office paper that could be separated, recycled and used again to produce more office paper, newsprint, paperboard and tissue papers. Implementing an office paper recycling program can be a way for businesses to reduce their solid waste disposal costs and even create a new source of revenue! By recycling, a business can show that it cares about the environment and can help foster a sense of pride and community involvement among its employees. The State of New Hampshire has initiated a sucessful office paper recycling program in all state agencies in order to help promote recycling throughout the state.

What Does a Business Need to Do to Establish an Office Paper Recycling Program?

Implementing an office waste paper separation and recycling program will vary in complexity depending on the size of the business. However, the secret to a successful program, whether it be quite simple or more complex, is to plan thoroughly and follow through carefully with each step. Listed below are some basic steps a business can use to get started.

1. *Establish a coordinator for the program.* The coordinator is the link between management, employees, maintenance supervisors and the waste paper buyer. This important position will be responsible for ensuring a smooth program implementation.

2. *Select a buyer.* Investigate potential markets to find a reputable waste paper buyer. This process will involve determining what materials the buyer will accept and in what quantities and requires negotiations to establish a good contract. The most acceptable types of waste paper are:

- letterhead paper
- typing paper
- high grade (bond) computer paper

- copy machine paper
- tablet paper

A good rule of thumb for determining waste paper quantities is to estimate that each employee that participates will produce about one-half pound of paper per day.

3. *Develop the separation and collection system.* Each employee begins the process by separating recyclable paper from other waste material and placing it in a desk-top container or folder. The employee then empties these containers into central collection receptacles which can be collected by janitorial personnel and transported to a central storage area. The waste paper buyer then picks up the material at this location.

4. *Announce the program to all employees.* Employee awareness and cooperation is essential for a successful recycling program. Several weeks before the recycling operation comes on-line, begin an education campaign that explains to employees the goals and methods of the program. This education campaign can include a "kick-off" poster or memo and brief orientation sessions to explain the program and stress the importance of each employee's participation.

5. *Monitor the program and circulate periodic reminders.* Monitoring and continued promotion are essential to publicize the success of the program and to sustain the employees' interest and participation. Issue memos, newsletters and announcements with updates on how the program is progressing.

A successful office waste paper recycling program will help ensure an adequate supply of waste paper for the manufacture of recycled products. Of equal importance is the need to demand products made from, or packed in, recycled materials. Businesses can have their company stationery, business cards and brochures printed on recycled paper stock. In this way, a business can help create an increased demand for recyclable waste paper.

Source: New Hampshire, Department of Environmental Services, "Technical Bulletin," 1990.

Appendix 6.4

DESIGNING A PUBLIC EDUCATION PROGRAM

For any recycling program to be successful and reach its maximum potential, a comprehensive public education program is required. Recycling represents a change in behavior for most people—therefore, a public education program must provide participants with the Information and the Motivation to change their behavior.

There are four principles a successful public education program needs to follow:

1. Identity—slogans, logs, themes, and mascots;
2. Consistency—information need to be on-going and correct;
3. Communication—flyers, newspaper articles, radio messages, etc., need to be easy to understand; and
4. Professionalism—everything from clever flyers to knowledgeable employees help to inform and motivate residents.

Getting Organized

Public education is more than a one person job. A well-rounded committee should be comprised of representatives from local government (including a person or department responsible for managing the recycling program), schools, local businesses, the hauler (if a private company will collect the recyclables), and interested citizens. Assign each committee member a specific task. For example:

- one person is responsible or issuing a press release each week for six weeks prior to the program's start-up date;
- another coordinates hanging posters around town with the program logo;
- someone volunteers to speak to students and local civic groups on how the program will work.

Remember, the recyling program's specifics should be finalized prior to any promotion to avoid last minute changes which can confuse residents.

Approach recycling as a marketing problem to solve, rather than just a topic of information to share. Like all marketing strategies, research is the foundation of a strong campaign:

- What do residents think about recycling?
- What kind of program would they participate in?
- If the program has been implemented, why are residents not participating?

Often, people want to recycle but are not sure how. A phone number residents can call to have their questions answered, such as the public works department or selectmen's office, is a good idea. Have answers to commonly asked questions handy for the folks answering the phone. Consistency and professionalism can't be spared at this level! The correct information needs to be given.

Spreading the Word

There are a variety of ways to educate residents about the recycling program, but remember to keep the information simple. In most cases, your objective is to motivate people to participate in the program. If you overload them with too much second and third phase information, you will loose them altogether. As the program progresses and residents become more knowledgeable, then share additional information on recycling to keep their interest, and their pride in the program.

Below are some examples of ways to inform and motivate residents:

Printed Materials — on Recycled Paper!
- Brochures and Fact Sheets
- Posters and Displays
- Slide and Video Presentations
- Supermarket Stuffers
- Reminder Calendars
- Newsletters

Free Media — Newpaper, Radio, Television
- Press Releases
- Feature Stories and Editorials
- Public Service Announcements
- Talk Show Opportunities
- Video Productions for Cable Television
- Video Cassettes for Training and Education

Paid Media
- Television
- Radio
- Newspapers

Community Outreach

- Public Surveys
- Door-to-Door Canvassing
- Billing Inserts
- Communicating with New Residents
- School, Church, Civic and Environmental Groups' Meetings and Publications
- Public Meetings and Workshops
- Telephone Recycling Hotline
- Block Leader Program

Don't be satisfied with a public education program just because it gets a lot of attention. Your measure of success is not how popular your advertisements are but how much your residents are recycling!

Conclusion

Though each community's recycling program is unique, there is no need to reinvent the wheel. Gather educational materials from other recycling programs, talk with committee members in neighboring towns to discuss their successes and failures. Videos, slide shows, and school curriculums already exist which you can use to educate residents.

Source: New Hampshire, Governor's Recycling Program, "Education Bulletin," December 1990.

Appendix 6.5

A SAMPLE RECYCLING BROCHURE

How to use the

Wilton Recycling Center

serving the towns of:

GREENFIELD, GREENVILLE
LYNDEBOROUGH, MASON, TEMPLE
and WILTON

Hours

Saturday 9:00 a.m. to 5:00 p.m.
Sunday 9:00 a.m. to 2:00 p.m.
Tuesday 1:00 p.m. to 5:00 p.m.
Wednesday 7:30 a.m. to 11:00 a.m.
Thursday 1:00 p.m. to 5:00 p.m.

* Open Thursdays until 7:00 p.m.
May 1 through September 30.
603-654-6150

Text:
Patricia H. Moore

Published by:
Wilton Board of Selectmen

PRINTED ON RECYCLED PAPER
at The Cabinet Press, Inc.

WILTON RECYCLING CENTER
Box 83
WILTON, NEW HAMPSHIRE 03086

TO:

History

The Recycling Center opened in August 1979 on the site of an old stone quarry. During the early part of this century the quarry was a popular swimming hole. In 1946 it became a dump for solid waste. Routinely the trash pile was set on fire in order to reduce volume, control odors, and contain rats.

In time the mountain of trash grew and the State authorities ordered the Town to cover the trash with a layer of sand. The polite term "sanitary landfill" was born.

In 1976 it became clear that the landfill could not continue in the long run.

The least expensive solution for the solid waste problem was to recycle as much as possible and incinerate or haul away what is left. It was equally evident that Wilton would not be able to bear the entire cost.

As a consequence, six towns banded together and agreed to share expenses as well as revenues proportionately on the basis of population.

The six towns also agreed to make separation of solid waste mandatory. This means that separation of the solid waste must be done before it reaches the Recycling Center.

	MATERIAL CATEGORIES	EXAMPLES	PREPARATION	#'S Refer to Questions Answered Page
CANS	ALUMINUM CANS	...soda & beer cans		
	TIN CANS	...soup & pet food cans	Rinse Food Cans	
	ALUMINUM FOIL	...pie plates	Remove Lables	
GLASS	GREEN GLASS	... beer & wine bottles		[1,2]
	CLEAR GLASS	..jars, clean window glass		[3,4]
	BROWN GLASS	.. liquor & beer bottles		
PAPER	CORRUGATED CARDBOARD & BROWN PAPER BAGS	...double walled cardboard		[6]
	MIXED PAPER	...school paper, junk mail cereal boxes, shoe boxes wrapping paper, catalogs		[7,8] [9,13]
	NEWSPAPER & MAGAZINES	...anything that comes with your newspaper	Keep Dry	[20,14]
PLASTIC	GREEN SODA BOTTLES	...plastic 7-up bottles	Remove Caps	[21]
	CLEAR SODA BOTTLES	...plastic coke bottles	Remove Caps	[14]
	STYROFOAM PACKING	...styrofoam p-nuts	Closed Box or Bag	[15]
	MILK JUGS	...cider, water & milk jugs	Rinse Jugs	[20,14]
METAL	SCRAP METAL	...appliances, tools, water heaters, pipes, ducting	Remove Non-Metal	[23]
	LOWGRADE & CONTAINER SCRAP METAL	...strapping, pails tail pipes, mufflers ferrous wire, tanks sealed containers, drums clothes hangers	Remove Non-Metal	
	ALUMINUM	.lawn chairs, license plates	Remove Non-Metal	
	COPPER	.copper pipe & wire	Remove Non-Metal	
	BRASS	. plumbing fixtures	Remove Non-Metal	
INCINERABLES	INCINERABLES *Recyclable items **must** be re-moved from incinerables. It is very expensive to incinerate materials. Glass & metal will damage the incinerator.* <u>*Keep your taxes low*</u> **RECYCLE!**	dirty or waxy paper, wet or dirty clothes, small pieces of furniture **small** amounts of shingles, used paper towels & plates, light-weight plastics, sanitary products plastic bags, toys, frozen juice cans, shoes, oil cans, rugs, baby diapers, rubber		[8,20] [7,14,6] [1,2,3,4]
	CONFIENTIAL PAPERS*	If your company has papers it wants incinerated instead of shredded	Call For Appointment	

LANDFILL	LANDFILL	small pieces of metal small amounts of sheetrock empty paint cans, **cold** ashes **dry** latex paint, **bagged** kitty litter, drinking glasses, light bulbs, couches, mattresses PVC pipe, aerosol cans, nails TV sets, ceramics	Dismantle furniture (as much as possible) to a manageable size	[11,19] [27,10,17]
	LANDFILL*	demolition waste non-household landfill		[19]
COMPOST	FOOD SCRAPS	..vegetable peelings, old food		[24,26]
	LEAVES & YARDWASTE	..clean wood shavings grass clippings, leaves		
WOOD	BRUSH & LUMBER	.. wooden building debris broken pallets, Christmas trees, vegetable crates window frames, chairs	Remove Non-Wood	[26,25] [29]
MISCELLANEOUS	TIRES* .... PALLETS .... AUTO BATTERIES .... WASTE OIL .... BOOKS .... WINDOWS & DOORS .... MISC. USEABLE ITEMS .... EYEGLASSES .... CLOTHING .... DEAD ANIMALS : by special arrangement only	..auto, truck, bicycle tires .sturdy whole pallets ..truck, auto & motorcycle ..crankcase oil, fat, grease ..hardcover, paperbacks .useable doors, windows .toys, dishes, items w/value .prescription glasses only .wearable clothing, rags Call to Arrange Disposal	In Non-Breakable containers w/Lids Unbroken Only Clean & Dry	[16] [18,30] [5]

WRC DOES NOT ACCEPT COMMERCIAL WASTE OIL
WRC DOES NOT ACCEPT LIQUID WASTE   [22]
WRC DOES NOT ACCEPT STUMPS (any wood over 5" in diameter)
WRC DOES NOT ACCEPT wood or brush on Mondays or Fridays.
WRC DOES NOT ACCEPT any mixed trash.
WRC DOES NOT ACCEPT 275 gallon oil tanks or 55 gallon drums.
WRC DOES NOT ACCEPT TOXIC WASTE including: pesticides, herbicides, asbestos, lead or other metal paints, drain cleaner, antifreeze, solvents, brake fluid, wood preservatives, rat poison, oven cleaner, old firearms, swimming pool chemicals, acids, photo chemicals, mercury or mercury batteries, epoxy, furniture stripper, any toxic waste or hazardous material.

* There is a charge to dispose of these items. Please see our policies list for rates.

191

POLICIES

DUMP PICKING - is allowed with permission only. If you find something of value you are expected to compensate the Recycling Center. The amount (if any) will be determined by the attendant in charge.

SEPARATION ORDINANCE - users of the Wilton Recycling Center are required by ordinance to separate trash, as outlined in this booklet. Changes may occur due to marketing needs. These changes will be publicized. Trash is subject to inspection and refusal by attendants. Repeated failure to separate trash correctly will result in a fine of $ 25 per pound (minimum fine $10.00).

HAZARDOUS WASTE - No hazardous or toxic materials will be accepted. The attendant in charge may refuse any material he/she believes could pose a threat to the Recycling Center, it's employees or the District. There will be an annual pick-up of household toxic waste. For information call 654-6150.

DISPOSAL CHARGES:

• over 1 cubic yard of demolition waste that must be landfilled	$40.00/C.Y.
• non-household landfill	$40.00/C.Y.
• tires	$ .50 each
• Confidential papers	$25.00/ bucketload (1/3 C.Y.)

ITEMS FOR SALE:

leaves and woodchips (customer loads)	free
leaves and woodchips (WRCloads)	
small pick-up truck	$10.00/load
large pick-up truck	$15.00/load
dump truck	$20.00/load
compost (customer loads) barrel	$ 1.00/barrel
small pick-up truck	$ 5.00/load
large pick-up truck	$ 7.00/load
compost (WRC loads)	
small pick-up truck	$10.00/load
large pick-up truck	$15.00/load
dump truck	$25.00/load
pallets	$ 1.00 each
windows and doors (donation or)	$ 1.00 each
books and useable items	donation

FEES ARE SUBJECT TO CHANGE!

COMMON QUESTIONS ANSWERED

1 Lids from glass bottles and jars go into landfill.
2 Pyrex, automobile (safety) glass and laboratory glass go into landfill.
3 Ceramics, broken dishes and mugs go into landfill.
4 Mirrors, light bulbs and drinking glasses go into landfill.
5 Eyeglasses are saved for the Lions Club.
6 Waxed cardboard or paper goes into incinerables.
7 Dirtypaper, napkins, paper towels, paper plates and disposable baby diapers go into incinerables.
8 Plastic grocery and dept. store bags go into incinerables.
9 Computer paper goes into mixed paper (special arrangements can be made for reimbursment for large quantities of computer paper).
10 Oil, lead and other metal based paints are unacceptable.
11 Latex paints should be air dried and put into landfill.
12 Newsprint flyers can go with newspapers.
13 Any paper you are not sure of put into mixed paper.
14 Plastic containers not listed go into incinerables.
15 Styrofoam packing material is available for sale.
16 Sturdy whole pallets should be set aside for Recycling Center use.
17 Wet or old yellowed newspaper can go into mixed paper.
18 Containers for waste oil disposal can be provided; ask attendant.
19 Small quantities of home demolition waste will be accepted free.
20 Bleach bottles and other household chemical bottles are unacceptable in milk jugs - put them into incinerables.
21 Base cups (on soda bottles) are acceptable; please remove caps.
22 The Recycling Center is a solid waste disposal facility and will not accept liquid waste.
23 All wood, plastic, upholstery, rubber etc. must be removed from scrap metal (plastic liners in appliances are OK; insulation in hot water heaters is OK).
24 Paper bags OK in food scraps.
25 Imbedded nails are OK in wood debris.
26 Large amounts of spoiled meat should be incinerated; call for appointment.
27 Empty paint cans go into landfill.
28 Copper wire does not have to be stripped.
29 No wood or brush will be accepted on Mondays or Fridays.
30 Commercial waste oil is un acceptable.

RECYCLING CAN BE CONFUSING AT FIRST; BUT ONCE YOU SET UP A SYSTEM IN YOUR HOME - IT'S EASY !!

Source: New Hampshire Resource Recovery Association, *Recycling in New Hampshire*, 1988, pp. 145–148.

Appendix 6.6

Newspaper, Cardboard, Magazines, & Mixed Paper

- Do you accept loose paper?
- Do you require a minimum amount, or pay a premium above a certain tonnage?
- Will you provide storage containers and/or transportation of paper?
- How much do you pay or charge for various grades of paper? Detail terms of payment or billing?
- Do you accept commingled materials? If so, what are the charges for tipping materials at your facility? How may the commingled material be collected and delivered?
- Please give the names of two or three current New Hampshire communities or businesses marketing low-grade paper through your company or program.

Container Glass

- What are your quality specifications for glass containers? Empty and rinsed? Color-separated? Whole or crushed? Are lids, bottle caps, and labels acceptable?
- Do you rent or sell containers for collection and/or provide transportation of glass to market?
- What are the options for transporting materials to your facility? Do you require a minimum amount to accept glass? Do you pay a premium above a given tonnage of glass?
- Will you provide copies of weight slips from certified scales?
- What will you pay (or charge) for glass? Please detail your terms for payment and/or billing.
- If you accept container glass commingled with other recyclables, describe which materials you will accept, how materials must be collected and delivered to your facility. What is the tipping fee for materials delivered to your facility?
- How long has your company been in the recycling business? Please give as references the names of two or three municipalities or businesses currently marketing glass through your firm.

Aluminum & Steel (Tin) Cans

- Must cans be washed?
- May steel and aluminum cans be commingled? Do you accept aluminum foil products in the mix? May empty aerosol containers and paint cans go in with the steel cans?
- Do you accept loose cans? May cans be crushed or flattened? Baled?
- Do you provide containers for collection of cans? Transportation of cans to market?
- What are you currently paying for cans? How are prices determined?
- Will you provide copies of weight slips from registered sales?
- How long has your company or program been in the recycling business? Give as references the names of two or three communities or businesses currently marketing aluminum or steel cans through your company.

Plastics — High Density Polyethylene (HDPE) and Polyethylene Terephthalate (PET)

- Which containers are acceptable?
- Must containers be separated by color? Rinsed? Flattened?
- Are caps, lock-rings, and labels acceptable?
- Do you offer any storage or transportation services?
- What do you pay or charge for HDPE and/or PET? Do you pay a premium for large volumes?
- If you accept commingled recyclables, list materials you will accept, and describe how materials must be collected and delivered to your facility. What is the tipping fee at your facility? Do you offer rebates from sales of materials?
- Will you provide copies of weight slips from certified scales?
- How long have you been in the recycling business? Please give as references the names of two or three municipalities or businesses currently marketing plastic through your firm or program.

Scrap Metal

- What materials do you buy and what are your specifications for these materials?
- Do you pay a premium for "clean" uncontaminated scrap metal?
- Do you provide containers for collecting metals? Transportation of loose materials to market?
- Do you offer on-site baling and marketing services?
- Do you provide your customers with copies of weight slips from registered scales?
- How long has your company been in the scrap recycling business? Give the names of two or three current accounts as references.

High-Grade Paper: Computer & Other Office Paper

- What specific materials may be included in each grade of paper you buy?
- Do you buy commingled office grades?

- Do you provide paper storage containers? Free or on a rental basis?
- Do you provide pick-up service? If so, what is the charge, if any, and how often can you service my site?
- Do you offer shredding services or a program of certified destruction of confidential documents?
- What are your current prices for various grades of office paper? Please detail your terms for payment.
- Will you provide copies of weight slips from registered scales?
- Do you offer a program for educating employees about office recycling?
- How long has your company been in the paper recycling business? Please give the names of two or three businesses who currently sell paper to your company.

Source: New Hampshire, Governor's Recycling Program, "Market Bulletins," M1, M2, M5, M7, 1990.

References

Apotheker, Steve. "Mixed Waste Processing: Head-To-Head with Curbside Recycling Collection." *Resource Recycling* 10 (September 1991): 33.

Chesterfield, N.H. *Annual Report.* 1989, 1990, 1991.

Duston, Thomas. "An Application of Cost-Benefit Analysis to Recycling." Paper presented at the American Public Health Association annual meeting, Chicago, October, 1989.

————. "The Microeconomics of Recycling." Paper presented at the Eastern Economics Association annual meeting, Pittsburgh, March, 1991.

Duston, Thomas, and Paula Stamps. "Success in Local Recycling: A Two-Year Evaluation." Paper presented at the American Public Health Association annual meeting, Atlanta, November, 1991.

Emerson Hospital. Personal correspondence between author and William Duston, director of finance. Concord, Mass., February 22, 1992.

Glenn, Jim. "MRF's in the U.S." *Biocycle* 32 (July 1991): 31–32, 34, 36–37, 74–77.

Keene, N.H. Ashuelot Valley Refuse District. "Hazardous Waste Day." April 28, 1990.

King, Lawrence W. "A Technical Study of Municipal Solid Waste Composting and the Effect of Disposable Paper Diapers." Cincinnati, Ohio: Procter and Gamble, 1991.

Mills, Edwin, and Phillip Graves. *The Economics of Environmental Quality,* 2d ed. New York: Norton, 1986.

National Soft Drink Association. "Things You've Always Wanted to Know about Soft Drink Container Recycling." Washington, D.C.: National Soft Drink Association, 1990.

New Hampshire. Department of Environmental Services. "Brokers, Processors and Markets for Recycled Materials." March 8, 1991.

————. "Technical Bulletins, WMD-1990-Fact Sheets." Concord, N.H., 1990.

New Hampshire. Governor's Recycling Program. "N.H. Recycling Equipment Bulletin E1." Concord, N.H., January 1991.

————. "State of New Hampshire Education Bulletin." Concord, N.H., December 1990.

———. "State of New Hampshire Market Bulletins." M1, M2, M3, M7, Concord, N.H., 1990.

———. Attachment to interdepartmental communication with Department of Economic Development. July 25, 1989.

New Hampshire Resource Recovery Association. *1991 Annual Report.* Concord, N.H., 1991.

———. 1992 Price List. Concord, N.H., 1992.

———. Recycling in New Hampshire: An Implementation Guide." Concord, N.H., 1988.

Phillips, Mark. "The Economics of Tire Burning." *Tire Review* (October 1991): 34, 50.

Smith, Vernon. "Dynamics of Waste Accumulation: Disposal versus Recycling." *Quarterly Journal of Economics,* (November 1972) 86:4.

Society of the Plastics Industry. "Percentage of Plastics by Type of Resin Used." *Plastics World,* (September 1989): 13.

———. "Package Design Will Be Shaped by Solid Waste." *Plastics World,* (April 1991): 21.

Spencer, Robert. "Taking Control of C&D Debris." *Biocycle,* 32:7 (July 9, 1991): 65.

Thompson, Stephanie. "Mandatory Recycling: The Pros and Cons." *American City and County,* (September 1991): 49, 50.

U.S. Environmental Protection Agency. Office of Solid Waste. *Recycle.* EPA/530-SW-88-050. Washington, D.C.: U.S. Government Printing Office, 1990.

University of Arizona Garbage Project. "Household Hazardous Waste." University of Arizona, 1988.

Windham, Vermont, Solid Waste Management District. Fee List. February 1, 1991.

Index

ABOUT THE AUTHOR

THOMAS E. DUSTON is currently Associate Professor of Economics at Keene State College of the University System of New Hampshire. He has a doctorate in economics as well as degrees in engineering, and paper mill management. He served as chairman of a committee which set up a recycling program in Chesterfield, New Hampshire, that is providing a 35 percent saving in the solid waste budget of that town. Various sections of the book have been well received when presented to professional audiences of the Eastern Economics Association and the American Public Health Association, as well as to state and local business and citizen's groups.